ISSUES THAT CONCERN YOU

Alternative Energy

Peggy Daniels Becker, *Book Editor*

GREENHAVEN PRESS
A part of Gale, Cengage Learning

GALE
CENGAGE Learning

Detroit • New York • San Francisco • New Haven, Conn • Waterville, Maine • London

Christine Nasso, *Publisher*
Elizabeth Des Chenes, *Managing Editor*

© 2010 Greenhaven Press, a part of Gale, Cengage Learning

Gale and Greenhaven Press are registered trademarks used herein under license.

For more information, contact:
Greenhaven Press
27500 Drake Rd.
Farmington Hills, MI 48331-3535
Or you can visit our Internet site at gale.cengage.com

For product information and technology assistance, contact us at

Gale Customer Support, 1-800-877-4253
For permission to use material from this text or product, submit all requests online at
www.cengage.com/permissions

Further permissions questions can be e-mailed to permissionrequest@cengage.com

Articles in Greenhaven Press anthologies are often edited for length to meet page requirements. In addition, original titles of these works are changed to clearly present the main thesis and to explicitly indicate the author's opinion. Every effort is made to ensure that Greenhaven Press accurately reflects the original intent of the authors. Every effort has been made to trace the owners of copyrighted material.

Cover image copyright Noah Golan, 2009. Used under license from Shutterstock.com.

LIBRARY OF CONGRESS CATALOGING-IN-PUBLICATION DATA

Alternative energy / Peggy Daniels Becker, book editor.
   p. cm. -- (Issues that concern you)
 Includes bibliographical references and index.
 ISBN 978-0-7377-4499-6 (hardcover)
 1. Renewable energy sources--Juvenile literature. I. Daniels, Peggy
TJ808.2.A57 2010
333.79'4--dc22

                                            2009044267

Printed in the United States of America
2 3 4 5 6 7 14 13 12 11 10

CONTENTS

Energy continues to be one of the most hotly debated topics in America today. Public discussion often focuses on issues related to Americans' use of fossil fuels such as oil, coal, and gasoline. With topics like gasoline prices and global warming in the news almost every day, Americans are also talking about alternative sources of energy that could replace fossil fuels. These alternative energies include solar, wind, and water power, and fuel made from trees, plants, and waste products. History tells us that these sources of energy, now viewed as alternatives, were once the primary sources of energy used by people to heat their homes, cook their food, and do their work. A look at the changing use of energy over time can help in understanding how Americans became dependent on fossil fuels and how earth's original sources of energy came to be seen as alternatives.

Using Energy

All of earth's life forms use energy to survive. In nature, plants and trees get energy from sunlight through the photosynthesis process. Energy from the sun and wind drive earth's water cycle, a critical support system for life. Wind energy helps the pollination process of some plants and trees and moves water on the surface of lakes and oceans to create waves. The energy of water moving in rivers and waterfalls is powerful enough to carve mountains into valleys and canyons and to carry rocks and soil to new locations. Earth itself is full of energy from its underground center of hot molten rock, which creates heat known as geothermal energy. All of these different types of energy work together to support life on earth.

Humans have always used earth's energy in one form or another, and the changing use of energy over time is closely related to the history of human civilization. The earliest human societies used wind, water, and solar energy long before the discovery of electricity, coal, or oil. The heat of sunlight was used to dry plants for food or fuel and to dry animal hides for clothing or shelter. For ancient Romans solar power was so important for heating buildings that they had laws preventing new structures from blocking an existing building's light. People used muscle power to do work, supplementing their own energy with horses, mules, and oxen for traveling, moving heavy loads, and pulling carts or plows. Then people built machines such as windmills to capture the energy of

An 1863 photo shows an oil field at Titusville, Pennsylvania. Along with coal and natural gas, oil would power the Industrial Revolution.

moving air and waterwheels to harness the energy of a flowing river or waterfall. These machines allowed people to do much more work than they could before.

It was not until the Industrial Revolution of the late eighteenth and early nineteenth centuries that people began to use fossil fuels as a primary source of energy. Coal, oil, and natural gas changed the way that people lived and worked. Within a period of only about one hundred years, the lives of most Americans were dramatically transformed by these new sources of energy. Prior to the Industrial Revolution, most Americans lived in rural areas and made their living by working on farms. Muscle power and fuel wood were the main sources of energy. With industrialization, job opportunities moved from agricultural work to manufacturing, shipping, construction, and so on. By the end of the 1800s, most Americans were living in cities powered by electricity, coal, and gas.

Coal and oil became even more important sources of energy as the nation expanded westward in the early 1900s. Large deposits of coal were discovered in the mountains and along the railroad routes that were being built at that time. Coal was used to make the iron and steel used in the construction of railroad tracks. It was burned as fuel in the steam engine locomotives that traveled the new railways. Coal was also burned for heat and to generate the electricity needed in homes and buildings. Around the same time, the discovery of a huge oil field in Texas increased the use of oil as an energy source, coinciding with the growing demand for automobiles.

Since the Industrial Revolution fossil fuels have continued to dominate America's energy usage. Although changes have occurred in areas such as home heating—for example, the coal furnaces that have been largely replaced by natural gas furnaces —fossil fuels still account for more than 80 percent of America's energy usage. For many years most of the fossil fuel needed to meet the country's energy demands was obtained from resources within the United States. But by the late 1960s, America's huge appetite for the energy needed to support modern lifestyles began to require more and more imported energy.

The 1960s also saw the beginning of the ecology movement, which brought attention to issues such as increasing pollution and the destruction of the natural environment. Around this time some Americans began to see fossil fuels as the root cause of these environmental problems. Then in the mid-1970s, a gasoline crisis caused prices to rise to record highs, and gas was rationed in some areas. People began to think more about America's dependence on imported energy, and the idea of alternative energy gained popularity.

Today a number of different factors have combined to increase interest in alternative energy. Concern for the natural environment, the American economy, and national security all play a part in the current debate on America's energy usage. Some people believe that continued reliance on imported oil places America at the mercy of other countries that control the supply and cost of fuel. Some economic experts have linked the high cost of imported energy with rising prices for necessities like food, clothing, and housing. And beyond these specific concerns about oil, a growing number of Americans believe that continued use of fossil fuels will result in global warming and extensive environmental damage.

Most Americans agree that energy alternatives are needed. Current public debate is focused on the best ways to reduce the use of fossil fuels and how to transition away from oil and coal toward energy alternatives. Some people believe that alternative energies such as wind, solar, and water power should be developed as a substitute for the coal used to make electricity. Others believe that biofuels or hydrogen fuel cells should be developed to replace the gasoline used in cars. Some scientists and energy experts say that these alternative sources of energy are less expensive than fossil fuels and better for the environment. But other experts say that more work needs to be done before any decisions can be made. Despite these differences of opinion, most energy experts agree that the future of U.S. energy will most likely include a mix of sources and a combination of many different technologies. A single energy solution may not meet every need or work the same way for every community.

In *Issues That Concern You: Alternative Energy*, authors debate these and other aspects of energy alternatives in excerpts from articles, books, reports, and other sources. In addition, the volume also includes resources for further investigation. The "Organizations to Contact" section gives students direct access to organizations that are working on the issues and technologies related to alternative energy. The bibliography highlights recent books and periodicals for more in-depth study, while in the appendix, "What You Should Know About Alternative Energy" outlines basic facts, and "What You Should Do About Alternative Energy" helps students use their knowledge to explore and evaluate various energy alternatives. Taken together, these features make *Issues That Concern You: Alternative Energy* a valuable resource for anyone researching this issue.

ONE

Changing to Alternative Energy Is Necessary

Ben Cipiti

Ben Cipiti is a researcher at Sandia National Laboratories. His work focuses on energy economics, fusion energy, nuclear fuel cells, and nuclear material safeguards. He is the author of *The Energy Construct*, a book exploring the creation of a clean, domestic, and economical energy future. In the following viewpoint Cipiti states that America's energy future will include more than one energy source. Cipiti examines the effectiveness of coal, natural gas, nuclear energy, and alternative energies such as wind power and solar power. He argues for the development of a national energy plan that uses a mix of traditional and alternative energies to meet America's future needs.

In the battle between climate change, energy policy, and capitalism the weakest voice at the table is that of the average person. While industrial lobbies have tremendous power in the government and while environmental organizations increasingly have more influence, somehow the voice of the average American has been missing from the discussion. But what does the ma-

Ben Cipiti, "Finding Middle Ground in Our Energy Future," *EnergyPulse.net*, April 18, 2008. www.energypulse.net. Copyright © 2002–2009, CyberTech, Inc. All rights reserved. Reproduced by permission of the publisher and the author.

jority of the population really want? Sure, we want to move toward clean energy, but we do not want to have to pay a tremendous amount for it.

With about 40% of our total energy use coming from oil and 50% of our electricity production coming from coal, we cannot eliminate our use of fossil fuels overnight or even in the next 20 years. With less than 4% of our energy use coming from non-hydroelectric sources of renewable energy, it could still take many decades for renewable energy to make a sizeable contribution. Our energy future will be made up of a combination of many technologies, and progress will only occur if we can learn to compromise on a mixture of clean energy options.

The Future of Coal and Natural Gas

As our most abundant fuel, coal will continue to be an important part of our energy mix for the next several decades. Probably one of the largest technical challenges of the next 20 years will be to

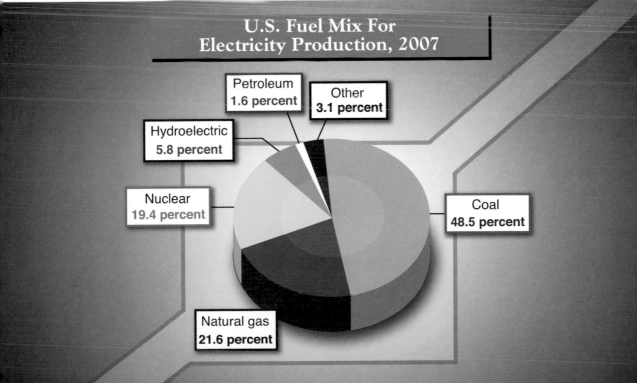

U.S. Fuel Mix For Electricity Production, 2007

Petroleum
1.6 percent

Other
3.1 percent

Hydroelectric
5.8 percent

Nuclear
19.4 percent

Coal
48.5 percent

Natural gas
21.6 percent

Taken from: Energy Information Administration, "Electric Power Annual: U.S. Electric Power Industry Net Generation," 2007.

figure out how best to sequester carbon dioxide from plant exhaust. And probably the greatest political battle of the next 20 years will be to get legislation in place to push for those technologies.

Natural gas produces about half the carbon dioxide as coal per unit of electricity produced, so it is unsure if future regulations will need to target this exhaust as well. Limited supplies of natural gas will limit how much we can depend on this fuel source. Due to the ability to bring gas turbines on line quickly for peak demand, it would make more sense to reserve gas use for this purpose. Other good uses of gas are to fill in the gaps in the reliability of renewable energy and for home heating, which has a very high efficiency. But it probably does not make sense to build base-load natural gas plants.

The Challenge of Limiting Carbon Emissions

A number of methods have been proposed to sequester and store carbon dioxide, but it will take strong support to test these technologies so that we may have viable options in 20 years. Carbon sequestration will depend entirely on passing new legislation due to the cost increases involved. Some projections show that a fully-sequestered coal plant would produce electricity for about the price of natural gas (given today's high gas prices). These plants take a hit on the overall efficiency by as much as 12 percentage points since it takes energy to sequester the carbon, but future designs may reduce that to only a 6 percentage point penalty.

Governments need to be careful enacting carbon legislation. Ideas like carbon taxes and the cap-and-trade system can lead to unintended side effects that the country may not be ready for. Previous experience in Europe has led to electricity price spikes and industries going out of business. Because we live in a global economy, such measures could increase demand for cheaper goods coming from countries with less stringent demands on pollution controls.

Instead, it may make more sense to limit emissions of plants similarly to how sulfur dioxide emissions have been limited in the past. It will take time to reduce the costs of carbon seques-

Developing ways to reduce carbon emissions as a means to prevent global warming is one of the great challenges of the next few decades.

tration technologies. Regulations should be enacted gradually to give industry time to adapt (and to prevent sharp price increases). For example, the first carbon legislation could mandate a 10% reduction in coal plant emissions that must be satisfied by implementing carbon sequestering technologies. If legislation like this is passed, industry will most definitely work to bring down the costs of the technology.

The Potential of Renewable Energy

The renewables are certainly a direction we want to move toward in the future, but cost and reliability will initially limit how quickly this sector will grow. A number of startups are around today in areas like solar and wind that could make a big difference in helping to drive down costs.

Solar continues to be one of the most expensive options for producing electricity, and some type of energy storage is needed to ensure a constant supply. Although its use is growing, for the near term significant cost reductions will still be required for wide-scale use. Even then, solar may only make sense in areas of the Southwest that receive plenty of sun.

Wind energy has the most potential for growth in the near-term since costs have decreased so much in the past couple of decades. In many areas of the country wind is very close to competitive: the push toward larger and more efficient designs will drop costs even more. However, as the portion of the power supply provided by wind gets larger, it becomes more difficult to deal with the low reliability of wind. It has been suggested that 20% is the maximum of a country's power supply that can come from unreliable sources.

The other key renewable energy options include biomass, geothermal, and hydro sources. Biomass will likely only continue to see smaller-scale use due to the large land requirements (and the high associated cost). Geothermal is limited by locations that are appropriate, and advanced systems that drill for geothermal energy will be expensive. Most of the hydroelectric sites have already been taken, and environmental groups have been pushing away from the building of dams. Wave and ocean current energy sources could be a large growth area in the future, but these technologies are at an immature point in their development today.

Of the renewables, wind energy is the most likely to expand significantly and could make up the majority of the renewable energy contribution. Hydroelectric, solar, geothermal, biomass, and ocean energy sources will all have a contribution, but their use will be limited over the next 20 years for the reasons outlined above. However, these energy sources may see more growth in the longer term.

Evaluating Nuclear Energy

The final piece of the puzzle is nuclear energy. Environmental groups are starting to embrace nuclear plants as the only way to achieve large-scale, emission-free power, but there is still some residual opposition to nuclear technologies.

The safety record of nuclear plants speaks for itself. The only major accident in our country, Three Mile Island, led to zero deaths and negligible radiation dose to the surrounding area. Compared to all other large-scale power plants, nuclear plants have the lowest death and injury rate per unit of electricity produced. When we factor in coal mining accidents, natural gas explosions, and hydroelectric dam ruptures, nuclear is in fact the safest. But often statistics mean little in light of fear of that which we may not understand.

Nuclear power does need strong leadership to figure out a final solution to dealing with nuclear waste. Since the fuel supply is somewhat limited, spent fuel will need to be reprocessed at some point in the future, but there is still time to develop these technologies. It may be difficult for some to choose nuclear, but energy demand is only increasing, and utilities need to build more plants. We need to be aware that opposing the building of a nuclear plant will most likely result in the building of another coal plant.

Using a Mix of Our Alternative Energies

With some compromise, we can achieve a much cleaner energy future that includes a diverse portfolio of energy technologies. The first piece of the pie is to focus on plug-in hybrids and electric vehicles to wean the country away from oil. Then coal and natural gas with carbon sequestration could provide a third of our energy use, nuclear power could produce a third, and the renewables could produce the final third.

Pushing renewables much beyond this level of development in the next 20 years is probably not possible in light of reliability limitations. Pushing nuclear beyond this level may not be possible due to political opposition. And one third of our energy use still coming from fossil fuels is probably realistic given our high dependency today.

There are many different ways to reach a diverse energy mix like this; the specific percentages are not important. What is important is that if we all cannot agree on this type of compromise, we may not make any progress at all.

TWO

Oil Independence Is Possible

Benjamin K. Sovacool

Benjamin K. Sovacool is a professor at Virginia Polytechnic Institute and State University and a research fellow at the National University of Singapore. His recent work focuses on the social barriers to renewable energy systems. He is the author of *Energy and American Society—Thirteen Myths*. In the following viewpoint Sovacool argues that the United States can achieve oil independence by 2030. He outlines the steps needed to reach that goal and describes the obstacles that must be overcome. Sovacool says that the government must enact policies to reduce American dependence on oil while also supporting the use of alternative energies.

Contrary to what most people might think, oil independence is possible for the United States by 2030.

The news is especially important when one considers that, between 1970 and 2000, economists estimate that the costs of American dependence on foreign supplies of oil have ranged between $5 and $13 *trillion* dollars. That's more than the cost of all wars fought by the U.S. (adjusted for inflation) going all the way back to the Revolutionary War.

Achieving Oil Independence

The trick is to start by thinking about oil independence a little differently. Oil independence should not be viewed as eliminating all imports of oil or reducing imports from hostile or unstable oil producing states. Instead, it should entail creating a world where the costs of the country's dependence on oil would be so small that they would have little to no effect on our economic, military, or foreign policy. It means creating a world where the estimated total economic costs of oil dependence would be less than one percent of U.S. gross domestic product by 2030.

Conceived in this way (and contrary to much political commentary these days), researchers at the Oak Ridge National Laboratory (ORNL) have calculated that if the country as a whole

One alternative to importing oil is to increase oil production in the United States.

reduced [its] demand for oil by 7.22 million barrels per day (MBD) and increased supply by 3 MBD, oil independence would be achieved by 2030 with a 95 percent chance of success. By reducing demand for oil, increasing its price elasticity, and increasing the supply of conventional and unconventional petroleum products, ORNL researchers noted that the country would be virtually immune from oil price shocks and market uncertainty. If large oil producing states were to respond to the U.S. by cutting back production, their initial gains from higher prices would also reduce their market share, in turn further limiting their ability to influence the oil market in the future.

Reducing Demand for Oil

So if decreasing American demand for oil by 7.22 MBD and increasing supply by 3 MBD would enable the U.S. to achieve oil independence in 2030, which combination of policies offers an optimal strategy? Policymakers, for instance, could lower demand for oil by making automobiles more efficient (by legislating more stringent fuel economy standards for light and heavy duty vehicles or lowering the interstate speed limit), promoting alternatives in mode choice (such as mass transit, light rail, and carpooling), or establishing telecommuting centers and incentives for commuters to work from home. They could also promote rigorous standards for tire inflation and reduce oil consumption in other sectors of the economy. Alternatively, they could increase alternative domestic supplies of oil, develop better technologies for the extraction of oil shale, mandate the use of advanced oil recovery and extraction techniques, and promote alternatives to oil such as ethanol, bio-diesel, and Fischer-Tropsch fuels [synthetic fuels].

Taken together, such policies could reduce demand for oil by 8.266 to 12.119 MBD and increase American oil supply by 8.939 and 12.119 MBD by 2030—well over the target set by the ORNL study. Thus, to insulate the American economy from the vagaries of the world oil market, policymakers need not focus only on geopolitical power structures in oil producing states. Instead, attempts to change the behavior of the country's automobile drivers, industrial leaders, and homeowners could greatly minimize reliance on foreign supplies of oil. To battle the "oil problem" policymakers need not talk only about sending more troops to Iraq or Saudi Arabia nor drafting new contracts with Nigeria and Russia. They could also focus on curbing American demand for oil and expanding domestic conventional and alternative supplies.

Removing Obstacles to Oil Independence

Such a synergistic approach would present immense obstacles. When President George W. Bush stated that "America is addicted to oil. . . . The best way to break this addiction is through technology," he was only partly right. Some of the tools required for oil independence have been around for decades, and instruments such as fuel economy standards and alternative fuels are well known. Getting them fully accepted is the challenge. Policymakers must move beyond the idea that technology will automatically solve the country's energy problems and come to address the remaining social, economic, and political barriers.

Instead of continuing to support mostly research and development on refining existing technologies and discovering new ones, one option could be to shift government support to efforts aimed at increasing public understanding of energy and transportation policy. The U.S. has already invested billions of dollars in basic and applied science, procurement, tax incentives, tax credits, subsidies, standards, and financial assistance to promote many of the options needed for oil independence. It may now be time to target the remaining social barriers in the same way the government has committed resources to promoting technological options.

Even if these remaining social barriers were somehow overcome, achieving oil independence would not be without costs. It would necessitate massive government investment and intrusion into the practices of industrial managers, automobile manufacturers, and the public at large. Even then, options such as

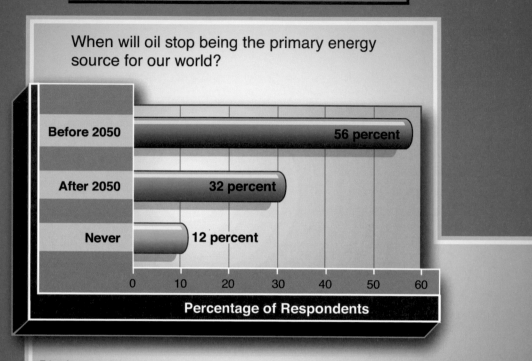

Most Americans Believe Oil Independence Can Be Achieved

When will oil stop being the primary energy source for our world?

Before 2050	56 percent
After 2050	32 percent
Never	12 percent

Percentage of Respondents

Taken from: www.forbes.com, "When Will Oil Cease to Be Our Primary Energy Source?" July 3, 2007.

more domestic drilling and wider use of coal-to-liquids would contribute to climate change and environmental degradation. More research is definitely needed to further assess these costs and benefits.

In essence, the debate over whether oil independence can be achieved for the U.S. continues only because those making policy continue to *believe* it cannot be achieved. The key to implementing a strategy of oil independence is more a matter of managing the *interdependence* of technologies available to reduce oil demand and increase supply, rather than trying to establish the *independence* of the United States from foreign supplies of oil. Once such interdependence is recognized and synergistically pursued, the country can achieve oil independence. The only remaining questions are how, and whether the benefits outweigh the costs.

THREE

Oil Independence Is Not a Realistic Goal

Paul Roberts

Paul Roberts is a contributing writer for *Mother Jones* and *Harper's Magazine* and the author of *The End of Oil*. In the following viewpoint Roberts argues that the United States cannot realistically hope to achieve independence from imported oil. He states that the United States would be better off working on energy security— gaining access to reliable, affordable, safe, and sustainable energy sources—and on energy conservation and more efficient energy usage. Roberts discusses many of the problems associated with alternative energies and outlines various other ways to reduce American oil usage. He identifies energy conservation as a global problem that requires commitment from many different countries working together toward the same goals.

What's not to like about energy independence?

In a word, everything. Despite its immense appeal, energy independence is a nonstarter—a populist charade masquerading as energy strategy that's no more likely to succeed (and could be

Paul Roberts, "The Seven Myths of Energy Independence: Why Forging a Sustainable Energy Future Is Dependent on Foreign Oil," *Mother Jones*, vol. 33, May/June 2008, pp. 30–37. http://motherjones.com. Copyright © 2008 Foundation for National Progress. Reproduced by permission.

even more damaging) than it was when [U.S. president Richard M.] Nixon declared war on foreign oil in the 1970s. Not only have we no realistic substitute for the oceans of oil we import, but many of the crash programs being touted as a way to quickly develop oil replacements—"clean coal," for example, or biofuels—come at a substantial environmental and political cost. And even if we had good alternatives ready to deploy—a fleet of superefficient cars, say, or refineries churning out gobs of cheap hydrogen for fuel cells—we'd need decades, and great volumes of energy, including oil, to replace all the cars, pipelines, refineries, and other bits of the old oil infrastructure—and thus decades in which we'd depend on oil from our friends in Riyadh [Saudi Arabia], Moscow [Russia], and Caracas [Venezuela]. Paradoxically, to build the energy economy that we want, we're going to lean heavily on the energy economy that we have. . . .

What America should be striving for isn't energy independence, but energy security—that is, access to energy sources that are reliable and reasonably affordable, that can be deployed quickly and easily, yet are also safe and politically and environmentally sustainable. And let's not sugarcoat it. Achieving real, lasting energy security is going to be extraordinarily hard, not only because of the scale of the endeavor, but because many of our assumptions about energy—about the speed with which new technologies can be rolled out, for example, or the role of markets—are woefully exaggerated. High oil prices alone won't cure this ill: We're burning more oil now than we were when crude sold for $25 a barrel. Nor will Silicon Valley utopianism: Thus far, most of the venture capital and innovation is flowing into status quo technologies such as biofuels. And while Americans have a proud history of inventing ourselves out of trouble, today's energy challenge is fundamentally different. Nearly every major energy innovation of the last century—from our cars to transmission lines—was itself built with cheap energy. By contrast, the next energy system will have to contend with larger populations and be constructed using far fewer resources and more expensive energy. . . .

Oil Independence Is Too Expensive to Achieve

Oil's qualities were unbeatable when it cost $25 a barrel, and even at $100, it still has a critical advantage. Because it was generated ages ago and left for us in deep underground reservoirs, oil exists more or less in a state of economic isolation; that is, oil can be produced—pumped from the ground and refined—without directly impinging on other pieces of the world economy. By contrast, many of oil's competitors are intimately linked to that larger economy, in the sense that to make more of an alternative (ethanol, say) is to have less of something else (food, sustainably arable land [land suitable for growing crops]).

Granted, oil's advantages will ultimately prove illusory due to its huge environmental costs and finite supply. But oil's decline won't, by itself, make alternatives any less problematic. Higher oil prices do encourage alternatives to expand, but in a world of finite resources, these expansions can come at substantial cost. Because good U.S. farmland is already scarce, every additional acre of corn for ethanol is an acre unavailable for soybeans, or wheat, whose prices then also rise—a ripple effect that affects meat, milk, soft drinks. . . . And for the record, to make enough corn ethanol to replace all our gasoline, we'd need to plant 71 percent of our farmland with fuelcrops. . . .

Energy Conservation Is a Better Solution

It should be clear not only that energy independence is prohibitively costly, but that the saner objective—energy security—won't be met through some frantic search for a fuel to replace oil, but by finding ways to do without liquid fuel, most probably through massive increases in energy efficiency. . . . Better energy efficiency is one of the fastest ways to reduce not only energy use, but pollution and greenhouse gas emissions: According to a [2008] study by McKinsey & Company, if the United States aggressively adopted more efficient cars, factories, homes, and other infrastructure, our CO_2 emissions could be 28 percent below 2005 levels by 2030.

And saving energy is almost always cheaper than making it: There is far more oil to be "found" in Detroit by designing more fuel-efficient cars than could ever be pumped out of ANWR [Arctic National Wildlife Refuge]. And because transportation is the biggest user of oil—accounting for 7 of every 10 barrels we burn—any significant reduction in the sector's appetite has massive ramifications. Even the relatively unambitious 2007 energy bill, which raises fuel-economy standards from 25 mpg to 35 mpg by 2020, would save 3.6 million barrels a day by 2030. And if we persuaded carmakers to switch to plug-in hybrids, we could cut our oil demand by a staggering 9 million barrels a day, about 70 percent of our current imports.

Such a shift would impose massive new demand on an electric grid already struggling to meet need, but plug-in hybrids actually stretch the grid's existing capacity. Charged up at night,

Plug-in hybrid cars can help to balance the electric grid by recharging at night when demand for electric power is low.

when power demand (and thus prices) are low, plug-in hybrids exploit the grid's large volume of unused (and, until now, unusable) capacity. Such "load balancing" would let power companies run their plants around the clock (vastly more cost-effective than idling plants at night and revving them up at dawn); as important, it would substantially boost the grid's overall output. According to the Department of Energy, with such load balancing, America's existing power system could meet current power demands and generate enough additional electricity to run almost three-quarters of its car and light-truck fleet. That alone would be enough to drop oil consumption by 6.5 million barrels a day, or nearly a third of America's current demand. . . .

Energy Conservation Is a Global Problem

Given America's reliance on imported oil, it seems safe to assume that if we succeeded in getting such dramatic reductions, whatever sacrifices we'd made would be more than compensated for by our new immunity to the nastiness of world oil markets. Let Saudi Arabia cut its production. Let [Venezuelan president] Hugo Chávez sell his oil to China. Such maneuvers no longer matter to Fortress America.

And yet, no country can really hope to improve its energy security by acting alone. True, cutting our own oil use would bring great things here at home, everything from cleaner air and water to lower noise pollution. But we'd be surprised by how little our domestic reductions changed the rest of the world—or improved our overall energy security.

The first problem, once again, is the small-planet nature of energy. America may be the biggest user of oil, but the price we pay is determined by global demand, and demand is being driven largely by booming Asia, which is only too happy to burn any barrel we manage to conserve or replace. Second, any shift to alternatives or better efficiency will take years and perhaps decades to implement. The U.S. car fleet, for example, turns over at a rate of just eight percent a year. That's as fast as consumers can afford to buy new cars and manufacturers can afford to make them, which means that—even in a fantasy scenario where the cars were already designed, the factories retooled, and the workers retrained—it would still take 12 years to deploy a greener fleet. . . .

The only way to achieve real energy security is to reengineer not just our energy economy but that of the entire world. Oil prices won't fall, evil regimes won't be bankrupt, and sustainability won't be possible—until global oil demand is slowed. And outside of an economic meltdown, the only way it can be is if the tools we deploy to improve our own security can be somehow exported to other countries, and especially developing countries. . . .

In the near term, however, the most practical energy export will be efficiency. China is so woefully inefficient that its economy uses 4.5 times as much energy as the United States for every dollar of output. This disparity explains why China is the world's second-biggest energy guzzler, but also why selling China more efficient technologies—cars, to be sure, but also better designs for houses, buildings, and industrial processes—could have a huge impact on global energy use and emissions.

As a bonus, such exports would likely be highly profitable. Japan, whose economy is nine times as energy efficient as China's, sees enormous economic and diplomatic opportunities selling its expertise to the Chinese, and America could tap into those opportunities as well—provided technologies with export potential get the kind of R&D [research and development] support they need. Yet this isn't assured. You may have read that the volume of venture capital flowing into energy-technology companies is at a record high. But much of this capital is flowing into known technologies with rapid and assured payoffs—such as corn ethanol—instead of more speculative, but potentially more useful, technologies like cellulosic ethanol. . . .

Energy Independence Is Not Possible

Given America's tectonic pace toward energy security, the time has come for tough love. Most credible proposals call for some

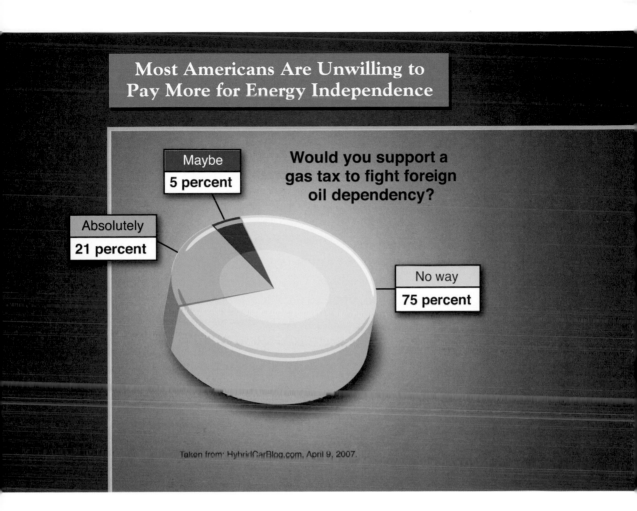

Most Americans Are Unwilling to Pay More for Energy Independence

Would you support a gas tax to fight foreign oil dependency?

Maybe
5 percent

Absolutely
21 percent

No way
75 percent

Taken from: HybridCarBlog.com, April 9, 2007.

kind of energy or carbon tax. Such a tax would have two critical effects. It would keep the cost of oil high and thus discourage demand, as it has in Europe, and it would generate substantial revenues that could be used to fund research into alternatives, for example, or tax credits and other incentives to invest in the new energy technologies. . . .

And higher energy taxes are just the first dose of bitter medicine America needs to swallow if it wants real energy security. For no matter how aggressively the United States cuts oil demand both at home and abroad, it will be years and perhaps decades before any meaningful decline. The 12-year fleet-replacement scenario outlined above, for example, assumes that efficient new cars are being mass-produced worldwide and that adequate new volumes of electricity can be brought online as the fleet expands—assumptions that at present are wildly invalid. A more reasonable timetable is probably on the order of 20 years.

During this transition away from oil, we will still need lots and lots (and lots) of oil to fuel what remains of the oil-burning fleet. If over those 20 years global oil demand were to fall from the current 86 million barrels a day to, say, 40 million barrels a day, we'd still need an average of 63 million barrels a day, for a total of 459 billion barrels, or almost half as much oil as we've used since the dawn of humankind.

And here we come to two key points. First, because the transition will require so much old energy, we may get only one chance: If we find ourselves in 2028 having backed the wrong clusters of technologies or policies, and are still too dependent on oil, there may not be enough crude left in the ground to fuel a second try. Second, even if we do back the right technologies, the United States and the world's other big importers will still need far too much oil to avoid dealing with countries like Iran, Saudi Arabia, and Russia—no matter how abhorrent we find their politics.

In one of the many paradoxes of the new energy order, more energy security means less energy independence.

FOUR

Biofuel Is a Good Alternative Energy Source

David Morris

David Morris is the cofounder and vice president of the Institute for Local Self-Reliance, which focuses on environmentally responsible community development practices such as local energy creation and ownership. In the following viewpoint Morris argues that biofuels, such as ethanol made from corn, are good alternatives to fuels made from oil. He describes how biofuel can fit into a national oil-independence strategy that includes multiple sources of energy and supports local economies. Morris concludes that better energy standards should be put in place by the government in order to encourage the development of biofuels.

In the last few years, the environmental position has shifted from an attack on ethanol from any source to an attack on corn and corn-derived ethanol. The assault on corn comes from so many directions that sometimes the arguments are wildly contradictory. In an article published in the *New York Times Magazine* earlier this year [2007] Michael Pollan, an excellent and insightful writer, argues that cheap corn is the key to the epidemic of obesity. The same month, *Foreign Affairs* published

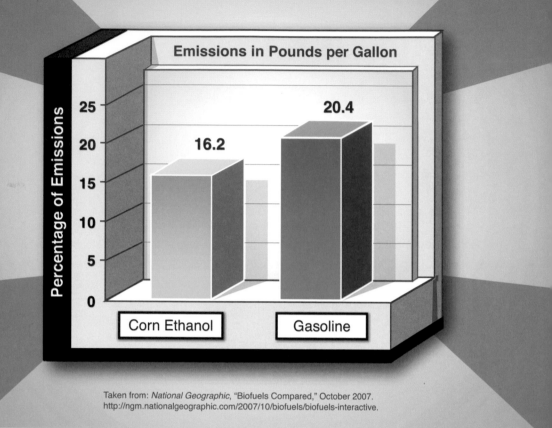

Biofuels Produce 22 Percent Fewer Greenhouse Gas Emissions

Emissions in Pounds per Gallon

Percentage of Emissions

16.2

20.4

Corn Ethanol

Gasoline

Taken from: *National Geographic*, "Biofuels Compared," October 2007.
http://ngm.nationalgeographic.com/2007/10/biofuels/biofuels-interactive.

an article by two distinguished university professors who argued that the use of ethanol has led to a runup in corn prices that threatens to sentence millions more to starvation.

Ethanol is not a perfect fuel. Corn is far from a perfect fuel crop. We should debate their imperfections. But we should also keep in mind the first law of ecology. "There is no such thing as a free lunch." Tapping into any energy source involves tradeoffs.

Yet when it comes to ethanol, and corn, we accept no tradeoffs. In 30 years in the business of alternative energy, I've never encountered the level of animosity generated by ethanol, not even in the debate about nuclear power. When it comes to ethanol, we seem to apply a different standard than we do when we evaluate other fuels. . . . I hope in the future we might engage in a more productive conversation and balanced discussion about the role of plants in a future industrial economy. To that end, I offer six propositions. I look forward to a debate on all or any one of these.

Biofuels Are Sustainable Fuel Sources

1. Sustainability requires molecules. Wind and sunlight are excellent energy sources, but they cannot provide the molecular building blocks that make physical products. For that we must choose minerals or vegetables (I'm lumping animals with vegetables for obvious reasons).

Minerals will always be an important source of molecules, in part because hundreds of billions of tons are already in existing products and these products have a very high recycleability potential. But ultimately we must increasingly rely on biological resources for our industrial needs if we are to achieve sustainability.

Plants Have Multiple Uses

2. Wind and sunlight can only be harnessed for some form of energy (thermal, mechanical, electrical). Plants, on the other hand, can be used for many purposes: human nutrition, animal feed, pharmaceuticals, chemicals, clothing, building materials, fuels. The challenge for public policy is to design rules that encourage the highest and best use of our finite land area (and sea and lake areas).

Few would [dispute] that human nutrition is the highest use of plants, followed by medicinal uses and possibly clothing. After that we might differ. My organization has argued that we should first use biomass to substitute for industrial products that use fossil fuels rather than for the fuels themselves. We make this argument in part because while there is insufficient biomass to displace a majority of fuels, there is a sufficient quantity to displace up to 100 percent of our petroleum and natural gas–derived chemicals and products. And these are much higher value products. . . .

Corn Has Played a Crucial Part
in the Biofuels Industry

3. Corn is a transitional energy feedstock, but it has played a crucial role in creating the infrastructure for a carbohydrate economy. We are moving beyond corn, to more abundant feedstocks like cellulose. But a carbohydrate economy, where plants have an industrial role, would have been delayed by 20–30 years if not for corn. . . .

We are nearing the end of the corn-to-ethanol era. Ethanol production has doubled since 2005 and promises to double again by 2010. It is unlikely any new corn-to-ethanol plants will be built beyond those currently in the construction pipeline. Even the National Corn Growers Association expects ethanol demand to exceed the capacity of the corn crop when all the new ethanol plants come online. All congressional bills that would increase the biofuels mandate also cap the amount of corn-derived ethanol at 15 billion gallons. After 2012, all additional ethanol capacity must be based on noncorn crops. . . .

Biofuels Can Reduce the Reliance
on Oil for Transportation

4. Electricity, not biofuels, will be the primary energy source for an oil-free and sustainable transportation system. But biofuels can play an important role in this future as energy sources for backup engines that can significantly reduce battery costs and extend driving range.

Even when we move from corn to cellulose, we likely lack sufficient arable land to cultivate enough biomass to displace more than about 25 percent of our transportation fuels (diesel plus gasoline). This is not an unimportant amount, but we need to accept that biofuels will not play the primary role in eliminating our dependence on oil. That role, as I've discussed in my 2003 report, *A Better Way to Get from Here to There*, will be played by electricity.

Miles traveled on electricity are oil-free miles because we use very little oil to generate electricity. Traveling on electricity

A plant in Scotland turns corn cobs into ethanol. The author says that in the future, biofuels will play an important part in reducing battery costs and extending driving range.

means getting over 100 miles per gallon equivalent, triple the increased fuel efficiency standard under debate in the U.S. Senate. Traveling on electricity generates no tailpipe pollution and costs 1–2 cents per mile compared to 10–15 cents per mile for traveling on gasoline or biofuels. The electricity would initially come from a grid system almost 50 percent powered by coal, but given the renewable portfolio standards in place, an increasing percentage of our electricity would come from renewable resources like wind or sunlight.

The Achilles' heel of all-electric cars is the cost and weight of batteries and the need for recharging every 100 miles or so. A backup engine overcomes that shortcoming. If the backup engine powers the car 25 percent of the time, we will have enough biomass to displace 100 percent of the petroleum used in the engine. Coupled with oil-free electricity, this can lead us to reduce by 80–100 percent our reliance on oil for transportation.

Biofuels Support Local Economies

5. Approach biofuels as an agricultural issue with energy security implications, not as an energy security issue with agricultural implications. Design policies to maximize the benefit to rural areas of using plant matter for industrial and energy uses. The key is local ownership of biorefineries. . . .

Local ownership benefits farmers in a number of ways. It allows them to hedge against crop price declines. If their crop price goes down, the input costs of the biorefinery also decline and all things being equal, profits will be higher and they will receive a higher dividend check at the end of the year. Studies by the Institute for Local Self-Reliance and other organizations have found that farmers can earn up to five times more per bushel by co-owning a biorefinery rather than simply selling to it.

Local ownership benefits rural areas, as many studies have documented, because a much greater portion of the dollar generated by the biorefinery stays within the community. Local ownership benefits state economies because it generates more taxable income.

Local ownership and the scale of biorefineries have never been a consideration of the environmental movement. That may be changing. Until recently, the organic agriculture movement, for example, focused on the biological health of the soil, not the economic health and security of the farmers and rural communities. Now in several states, organic certification takes into account ownership and place. A new slogan is "Local is the new organic." . . .

Performance Standards for Biofuel Are Needed

6. Support performance, not prescriptive, standards.

Performance standards specify outcomes. They specify an end result, but not how that result is achieved. They focus on ends and leave the design of means to entrepreneurs. Performance standards foster competition and innovation. Renewable electricity portfolio standards, now in place in two dozen states, are performance standards. A variety of renewable fuels qualify —wind, solar, biomass, hydro, geothermal, landfill gas, ocean or tidal power.

Prescriptive standards are like a recipe. They prescribe exactly how to achieve a specific result. The 2005 federal renewable fuel standard for transportation fuels and the new standard under debate in the U.S. Senate are prescriptive standards. They mandate the use of a single renewable fuel: ethanol.

Congress should transform the renewable transportation fuel standard into a performance standard, not only for internal consistency, but also because of the coming convergence of electricity and transportation. . . .

Wind energy accounts for 80 percent to 95 percent of the renewable electricity generated under the renewable portfolio standards. Because of their head start, national delivery systems and drop in capability to existing engines, ethanol and biodiesel would comprise at least as high a proportion of a renewable transportation fuel performance standard in the near future.

But in the longer term, a performance standard is superior public policy. It mandates ends, not means. It encourages diversity and flexibility and innovation, and provides a level playing field for entrepreneurs.

FIVE

Biofuel Is Not a Good Alternative Energy Source

Eric Holt-Giménez

Eric Holt-Giménez is the executive director of the Food First/Institute for Food and Development Policy. He is the author of *Campesino a Campesino: Voices from Latin America's Farmer to Farmer Movement for Sustainable Agriculture*. In the following viewpoint Holt-Giménez presents the argument that the biofuel industry is responsible for a growing food shortage in much of the world. He explains that farmland is being converted from growing food crops to growing crops for use in making biofuels. He provides details about all of the problems this conversion is causing and calls for a reduction in biofuel production until more government regulations can be put in place.

Biofuels invoke an image of renewable abundance that allows industry, politicians, the World Bank, the UN [United Nations], and even the Intergovernmental Panel on Climate Change to present fuel from corn, sugarcane, soy and other crops as a smooth transition from peak oil to a renewable fuel economy. Myths of abundance divert attention away from powerful economic interests that benefit from this biofuels transition, avoiding discussion of the growing price that citizens of the Global South are beginning to pay to maintain the consumptive oil-based lifestyle of the North. Biofuels mania obscures the profound consequences of the industrial transformation of our food and fuel systems—The Agro-fuels Transition. . . .

Agro-fuel champions assure us that because fuel crops are renewable, they are environmentally friendly, can reduce global warming, and will foster rural development. But the tremendous market power of agro-fuel corporations, coupled with weak political will of governments to regulate their activities, is a recipe for environmental disaster and increasing hunger in the Global South. It's time to examine the myths fueling this agro-fuel boom—before it's too late.

Brazilian sugarcane is trucked to an ethanol-producing plant. Land that could be used for food production is now being used for biofuel production, causing food shortages in some countries.

Biofuel Crops Harm the Environment

Because photosynthesis from fuel crops removes greenhouse gases from the atmosphere and can reduce fossil fuel consumption, we are told fuel crops are green. But when the full "life cycle" of agro-fuels is considered—from land clearing to automotive consumption—the moderate emission savings are undone by far greater emissions from deforestation, burning, peat drainage, cultivation, and soil carbon losses. Every ton of palm oil produced results in 33 tons of carbon dioxide emissions—10 times more than petroleum. Tropical forests cleared for sugarcane ethanol emit 50% more greenhouse gasses than the production and use of the same amount of gasoline. Commenting on the global carbon balance, Doug Parr, chief UK [United Kingdom] scientist at Greenpeace states flatly, "If even five percent of biofuels are sourced from wiping out existing ancient forests, you've lost all your carbon gain." . . .

Proponents of agro-fuels argue that fuel crops planted on ecologically degraded lands will improve, rather than destroy, the environment. Perhaps the government of Brazil had this in mind when it re-classified some 200 million hectares [1 hectare = about 2.5 acres] of dry tropical forests, grassland, and marshes as "degraded" and apt for cultivation. In reality, these are the bio-diverse ecosystems of the Mata Atlantica, the Cerrado, and the Pantanal, occupied by indigenous people, subsistence farmers, and extensive cattle ranches. The introduction of agro-fuel plantations will simply push these communities to the "agricultural frontier" of the Amazon where deforestation will intensify. . . .

Biofuel Crops Hurt Farming Communities

In the tropics, 100 hectares dedicated to family farming generates 35 jobs. Oil palm and sugarcane provide 10 jobs, eucalyptus two, and soybeans just one half-job per 100 hectares, all poorly paid. Until this boom, agro-fuels primarily supplied local markets, and even in the U.S., most ethanol plants were small and farmer-owned. Big Oil, Big Grain, and Big Genetic Engineering are rapidly consolidating control over the entire agro-fuel value chain.

The market power of these corporations is staggering: Cargill and ADM [Archer Daniels Midland] control 65% of the global grain trade, Monsanto and Syngenta a quarter of the $60 billion gene-tech industry. This market power allows these companies to extract profits from the most lucrative and low-risk segments of the value chain—selling inputs, processing and distributing. Agrofuels growers will be increasingly dependent on this global oligopoly of companies. Farmers are not likely to receive many benefits. Smallholders will likely be forced off the land. Hundreds of thousands have already been displaced by the soybean plantations in a 50+ million hectare area covering southern Brazil, northern Argentina, Paraguay, and eastern Bolivia.

Biofuel Crops Increase World Hunger

Hunger, said [Nobel Prize–winning economist] Amartya Sen , results not from scarcity, but poverty. According to the FAO [the UN's Food and Agriculture Organization], there is enough food in the world to supply everyone with a daily 3,200-calorie diet of fresh fruit, nuts, vegetables, dairy and meat. Nonetheless, because they are poor, 824 million people continue to go hungry. In 1996, world leaders promised to halve the number of hungry people living in extreme poverty by 2015. Little progress has been made. The world's poorest people already spend 50–80% of their total household income on food. They suffer when high fuel prices push up food prices. Now, because food and fuel crops are competing for land and resources, high food prices may actually push up fuel prices. Both increase the price of land and water. This perverse, inflationary spiral puts food and productive resources out of reach for the poor. The International Food Policy Research Institute has estimated that the price of basic food staples will increase 20–33% by the year 2010 and 26–135% by the year 2020. Caloric consumption typically declines as price rises by a ratio of 1:2. With every one percent rise in the cost of food, 16 million people are made food insecure. If current trends continue, some 1.2 billion people could be chronically hungry by 2025—600 million more than previously predicted. World food aid will not likely come to

Biofuel Crops Reduce World Food Supply

The amount of corn used to create enough biofuel to fill one SUV gas tank just one time would feed one person for an entire year.

Taken from: *The Globalist*, "Starving for Fuel: How Ethanol Production Contributes to Global Hunger," August 2, 2006. www.theglobalist.com/storyid.aspx?StoryID=5518.

the rescue because surpluses will go into our gas tanks. What is urgently needed is massive transfers of food-producing resources to the rural poor; not converting land to fuel production.

Faith in Unproven "Second-Generation" Biofuels Is Misplaced

Proponents of agro-fuels argue that present agro-fuels made from food crops will soon be replaced with environmentally-friendly crops like fast-growing trees and grasses. This myth, wryly referred to as the "bait and switchgrass" shell game, makes food-based fuels socially acceptable.

The agro-fuel transition transforms land use on a massive scale, pitting food production against fuel production for land, water and resources. The issue of which crops are converted to fuel is irrelevant. Wild plants cultivated as fuel crops won't have a smaller "environmental footprint." They will rapidly migrate from hedgerows and woodlots onto arable lands to be intensively cultivated like any other industrial crop, with all the associated environmental externalities. . . .

Cellulosic ethanol, a product that has yet to demonstrate any carbon savings, is unlikely to replace agro-fuel within the next five to eight years—in time to avoid the worst impacts of global warming. Major breakthroughs in plant physiology that permit the economically efficient breakdown of cellulose, hemicellulose, and lignin are required. Industry is either betting on miracles or counting on taxpayer bail-outs. Faith in science is not science. Selective faith in unproven and possibly unattainable second-generation biofuel—rather than working to improve existing solar, wind, or conservation technologies—is a bias in favor of agro-fuel giants.

Biofuel Is Not a Good Alternative Energy

The International Energy Agency estimates that over the next 23 years, the world could produce as much as 147 million tons of agro-fuel. This will be accompanied by a lot of carbon, nitrous oxide, erosion, and over 2 billion tons of waste water. Remarkably, this fuel will barely offset the yearly increase in global oil demand, now standing at 136 million tons a year—not offsetting any of the existing demand. . . .

Government-subsidies and mandated targets for agro-fuels are the perfect answer to [the current] slump in agribusiness profits, growing as oil shrinks, and concentrating market power in the hands of the most powerful players in the food and fuel industries. Like the original Agrarian Transition, the present Agro-fuels Transition will "enclose the commons" by industrializing the remaining forests and prairies of the world. It will drive the planet's remaining smallholders, family farmers, and indigenous peoples to the cities. This government-industry collusion has the potential to funnel rural resources to urban centers in the form of fuel, concentrating industrial wealth. But it may push millions of people into poverty and increase starvation-related deaths dramatically. . . .

Limits—not incentives—must be placed on the agro-fuels industry. If agro-fuels are to be forest and food friendly, grain, cane, and oil-palm industries require strong global management, regulation and enforcement. Strong, enforceable standards based on limiting land planted to agro-fuels are urgently needed, as are anti-trust laws powerful enough to prevent further corporate concentration. Sustainable benefits to the countryside will only accrue if agro-fuels complement local, regional and national plans for sustainable rural development.

Biofuel Production Should Be Slowed

The Agro-fuels Transition is not inevitable. There is no inherent reason to sacrifice sustainable, equitable food and fuel systems to industry. Many successful, locally-focused, energy-efficient and people-centered alternatives are presently producing food and fuel in ways that do not threaten food systems, the environment, or livelihoods. The question is not whether ethanol and bio-diesel have a place in our future, but whether or not we allow a handful of global corporations to impoverish the planet and the majority of its people. To avoid this trap we must promote a steady-state agrarian transition built on re-distributive land reform that repopulates and stabilizes the world's struggling rural communities. This includes rebuilding and strengthening our local food systems, and creating conditions for the local re-investment of rural wealth. Putting people and environment—instead of corporate mega-profits—at the center of rural development requires food sovereignty: the right of people to determine their own food systems. . . .

Time and public debate is needed to assess the potential impacts of agro-fuels, and to develop the regulatory structures, programs, and incentives for conservation and food and fuel development alternatives. We need the time to forge a better transition—an agrarian transition for both food and fuel sovereignty.

SIX

Nuclear Power Is a Good Alternative Energy Source

Patrick Moore

Patrick Moore is the cofounder of environmental activism organization Greenpeace and the cochair of the Clean and Safe Energy Coalition, which supports increased use of nuclear energy. In the following viewpoint Moore explains that while he was once opposed to the use of nuclear energy, he has since changed his mind and now supports nuclear power as a good alternative energy. Moore outlines several popular objections to the use of nuclear power and explains what has been done to overcome the risks associated with it. He argues that nuclear energy is the best alternative to energy from coal and oil, and he encourages environmental activists to rethink their positions on nuclear power.

In the early 1970s when I helped found Greenpeace, I believed that nuclear energy was synonymous with nuclear holocaust, as did most of my compatriots. That's the conviction that inspired Greenpeace's first voyage up the spectacular rocky northwest coast to protest the testing of U.S. hydrogen bombs in Alaska's Aleutian Islands. Thirty years on, my views have changed, and the rest of the environmental movement needs to

Patrick Moore, "Going Nuclear: A Green Makes the Case," *Washington Post*, April 16, 2006. www.washingtonpost.com. Reproduced by permission of the author.

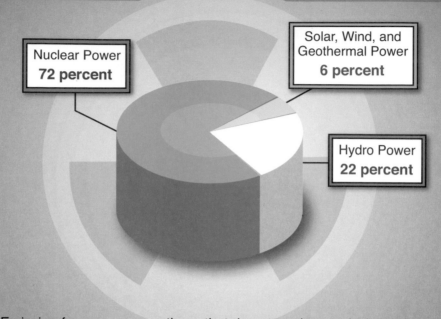

Nuclear Energy Is the Largest Source of Emission-Free Electricity

Nuclear Power
72 percent

Solar, Wind, and Geothermal Power
6 percent

Hydro Power
22 percent

Emission-free sources are those that do not produce emissions of carbon dioxide (CO_2), nitrogen oxides (NO_x), or sulfur dioxide (SO_2).

Taken from: Nuclear Energy Institute, "Sources of Emission-Free Electricity InfoGraphic," 2008.

update its views, too, because nuclear energy may just be the energy source that can save our planet from another possible disaster: negative impacts from climate change.

Look at it this way: More than 600 coal-fired electric plants in the United States produce 36 percent of U.S. emissions—or nearly 10 percent of global emissions—of CO_2, the primary greenhouse gas responsible for climate change. Nuclear energy is the only large-scale, cost-effective energy source that can reduce these emissions while continuing to satisfy a growing demand for power. And these days it can do so safely.

I say that guardedly, of course, just days after Iranian President Mahmoud Ahmadinejad announced [on April 11, 2006] that his country had enriched uranium. "The nuclear technology is only for the purpose of peace and nothing else," he said. But there is widespread speculation that, even though the process is ostensibly dedicated to producing electricity, it is in fact a cover for building nuclear weapons.

And although I don't want to underestimate the very real dangers of nuclear technology in the hands of rogue states, we cannot simply ban every technology that is dangerous. That was the all-or-nothing mentality at the height of the Cold War, when anything nuclear seemed to spell doom for humanity and the environment. In 1979, Jane Fonda and Jack Lemmon produced a frisson [shiver] of fear with their starring roles in "The China Syndrome," a fictional evocation of nuclear disaster in which a reactor meltdown threatens a city's survival. Less than two weeks after the blockbuster film opened, a reactor core meltdown at Pennsylvania's Three Mile Island nuclear power plant sent shivers of very real anguish throughout the country.

Nuclear Power Is Safe

What nobody noticed at the time, though, was that Three Mile Island was in fact a success story: The concrete containment structure did just what it was designed to do—prevent radiation from escaping into the environment. And although the reactor itself was crippled, there was no injury or death among nuclear workers or nearby residents. Three Mile Island was the only serious accident in the history of nuclear energy generation in the United States, but it was enough to scare us away from further developing the technology: There hasn't been a nuclear plant ordered up since then.

Today, there are 103 nuclear reactors quietly delivering just 20 percent of America's electricity. Eighty percent of the people living within 10 miles of these plants approve of them (that's not including the nuclear workers). Although I don't live near a nuclear plant, I am now squarely in their camp.

And I am not alone among seasoned environmental activists in changing my mind on this subject. British atmospheric scientist James Lovelock, father of the Gaia theory, believes that nuclear energy is the only way to avoid adverse consequences from climate change. Stewart Brand, founder of the "Whole Earth

Catalog," says the environmental movement must embrace nuclear energy to wean ourselves from fossil fuels. On occasion, such opinions have been met with excommunication from the anti-nuclear priesthood: The late British Bishop Hugh Montefiore, founder and director of Friends of the Earth, was forced to resign from the group's board after he wrote a pro-nuclear article in a church newsletter.

There are signs of a new willingness to listen, though, even among the staunchest anti-nuclear campaigners. When I attended the Kyoto climate meeting in Montreal last December [2005], I spoke to a packed house on the question of a sustainable energy future. I argued that the only way to reduce fossil fuel emissions from electrical production is through an aggressive program of renewable energy sources (hydroelectric, geothermal heat pumps, wind, etc.) plus nuclear. The Greenpeace spokesperson was first at the mike for the question period, and I expected a tongue-lashing. Instead, he began by saying he agreed with much of what I said—not the nuclear bit, of course, but there was a clear feeling that all options must be explored.

Here's why: Wind and solar power have their place, but because they are intermittent and unpredictable they simply can't replace big baseload plants such as coal, nuclear and hydroelectric. Natural gas, a fossil fuel, is too expensive already, and its price is too volatile to risk building big baseload plants. Given that hydroelectric resources are built pretty much to capacity, nuclear is, by elimination, the only viable substitute for coal. It's that simple.

Responding to Fear of Nuclear Power

That's not to say that there aren't real problems—as well as various myths—associated with nuclear energy. Each concern deserves careful consideration:

Nuclear energy is expensive. It is in fact one of the least expensive energy sources. In 2004, the average cost of producing nuclear energy in the United States was less than two cents per kilowatt-hour, comparable with coal and hydroelectric. Advances in technology will bring the cost down further in the future.

The author says that the fear caused by America's only serious nuclear accident, at Three Mile Island (pictured), is the primary reason that no U.S. nuclear plants have been built since the accident.

Nuclear plants are not safe. Although Three Mile Island was a success story, the accident at Chernobyl, 20 years ago this month, was not. But Chernobyl was an accident waiting to happen. This early model of Soviet reactor had no containment vessel, was an inherently bad design and its operators literally blew it up. The multi-agency U.N. Chernobyl Forum reported last year that 56 deaths could be directly attributed to the accident, most of those from radiation or burns suffered while fighting the fire. Tragic as those deaths were, they pale in comparison to the more than 5,000 coal-mining deaths that occur worldwide every year. No one has died of a radiation-related accident in the history of the U.S. civilian nuclear reactor program. (And although hundreds of uranium mine workers did die from radiation exposure underground in the early years of that industry, that problem was long ago corrected.)

Nuclear waste will be dangerous for thousands of years. Within 40 years, used fuel has less than one-thousandth of the radioactivity it had when it was removed from the reactor. And it is incorrect to call it waste, because 95 percent of the potential energy is still contained in the used fuel after the first cycle. Now that the United States has removed the ban on recycling used fuel, it will be possible to use that energy and to greatly reduce the amount of waste that needs treatment and disposal. Last month, Japan joined France, Britain and Russia in the nuclear-fuel-recycling business. The United States will not be far behind.

Nuclear reactors are vulnerable to terrorist attack. The six-feet-thick reinforced concrete containment vessel protects the contents from the outside as well as the inside. And even if a jumbo jet did crash into a reactor and breach the containment, the reactor would not explode. There are many types of facilities that are far more vulnerable, including liquid natural gas plants, chemical plants and numerous political targets.

Nuclear fuel can be diverted to make nuclear weapons. This is the most serious issue associated with nuclear energy and the most difficult to address, as the example of Iran shows. But just because nuclear technology can be put to evil purposes is not an argument to ban its use.

Nuclear Power in Context

Over the past 20 years, one of the simplest tools—the machete—has been used to kill more than a million people in Africa, far more than were killed in the Hiroshima and Nagasaki nuclear bombings combined. What are car bombs made of? Diesel oil, fertilizer and cars. If we banned everything that can be used to kill people, we would never have harnessed fire.

The only practical approach to the issue of nuclear weapons proliferation is to put it higher on the international agenda and to use diplomacy and, where necessary, force to prevent countries or terrorists from using nuclear materials for destructive ends. And new technologies such as the reprocessing system recently introduced in Japan [in March 2006] (in which the plutonium is never separated from the uranium) can make it much more difficult for terrorists or rogue states to use civilian materials to manufacture weapons.

The 600-plus coal-fired plants emit nearly 2 billion tons of CO_2 annually—the equivalent of the exhaust from about 300 million automobiles. In addition, the Clean Air Council reports that coal plants are responsible for 64 percent of sulfur dioxide emissions, 26 percent of nitrous oxides and 33 percent of mercury emissions. These pollutants are eroding the health of our environment, producing acid rain, smog, respiratory illness and mercury contamination.

Meanwhile, the 103 nuclear plants operating in the United States effectively avoid the release of 700 million tons of CO_2 emissions annually—the equivalent of the exhaust from more than 100 million automobiles. Imagine if the ratio of coal to nuclear were reversed so that only 20 percent of our electricity was generated from coal and 60 percent from nuclear. This would go a long way toward cleaning the air and reducing greenhouse gas emissions. Every responsible environmentalist should support a move in that direction.

SEVEN

Nuclear Power Is Risky and Expensive

Christian Parenti

> Christian Parenti is a frequent contributor to *The Nation*. In the following viewpoint Parenti provides an overview of the problems associated with nuclear energy. He focuses on the high cost and many risks of generating nuclear power and the problem of radioactive nuclear waste. Parenti argues that current support for nuclear power is being driven by the advertising agency hired by the nuclear industry. Parenti also argues that nuclear power is a distraction that is keeping the nation from pursuing better approaches to alternative energy.

If you listen to the rhetoric, nuclear power is back. . . .

The fact is, nuclear power has not recovered from the crisis that hit it three decades ago with the reactor fire at Browns Ferry, Alabama, in 1975 and the meltdown at Three Mile Island in 1979. Then came what seemed to be the coup de grâce: Chernobyl in 1986. The last nuclear power plant ordered by a US utility, the TVA's Watts Bar 1, began construction in 1973 and took twenty-three years to complete. Nuclear power has been in steady decline worldwide since 1984, with almost as many plants canceled as completed since then. . . .

Christian Parenti, "What Nuclear Renaissance?" *Nation*, vol. 286, May 12, 2008, pp. 11–14.

Nuclear Power Is Expensive

The fundamental fact is that nuclear power is too expensive and risky to attract the necessary commercial investors. Even with vast government subsidies, it is difficult or almost impossible to get proper financing and insurance. The massive federal subsidies on offer will cover up to 80 percent of construction costs of several nuclear power plants in addition to generous production tax credits, as well as risk insurance. But consider this: the average two-reactor nuclear power plant is estimated to cost $10 billion to $18 billion to build. That's before cost overruns, and no US nuclear power plant has ever been delivered on time or on budget. . . .

Another reason atomic energy is so expensive is that its accidents are potentially catastrophic, and activists have forced utilities to build in costly double and triple safety systems. Right-wing champions of atom-smashing blame prohibitive costs on neurotic fears and unnecessary safety measures. They have a point in that safety is expensive, but safety is hardly excessive—details on that in a moment.

More important is the fact that nuclear fission is a mind-bogglingly complex process, a sublime, truly Promethean technology. Let's recall: it involves smashing a subatomic particle, a neutron, into an atom of uranium-235 to release energy and more neutrons, which then smash other atoms that release more energy and so on infinitely, except the whole process is controlled and used to boil water, which spins a turbine that generates electricity.

In this nether realm, where industry and science seek to reproduce a process akin to that which occurs inside the sun, even basic tasks—like moving the fuel rods, changing spare parts—become complicated, mechanized and expensive. Atom-smashing is to coal power, or a windmill, as a Formula One race-car engine is to the mechanics of a bicycle. Thus, it costs an enormous amount of money.

Worldwide, about twenty nuclear power plants are being built, but most are in Asia and Russia and are closely linked to nuclear weapons programs. Japan and France have large nuke programs, but both countries heavily subsidize their plants, use a single design and built their fleets not to make profits but to ensure some minimum strategic energy independence and, for France, to build an atomic arsenal.

Even if a society were ready to absorb the high costs of nuclear power, it hardly makes the most sense as a tool to quickly combat climate change. These plants take too long to build. A 2004 analysis in *Science* by Stephen Pacala and Robert Socolow, of Princeton University's Carbon Mitigation Initiative, estimates that achieving just one-seventh of the carbon reductions necessary to stabilize atmospheric CO_2 at 500 parts per billion would require "building about 700 new 1,000-megawatt nuclear plants around the world." That represents a huge wave of investment that few seem willing to undertake, and it would require decades to accomplish. . . .

Support for Nuclear Energy Is Questionable

The notion that nukes make sense and are the version of green preferred by grown-ups is being conjured by a slick PR [public relations] campaign. The Nuclear Energy Institute—the industry's main trade group—has retained [PR firm] Hill and Knowlton to run a greenwashing campaign.

Part of their strategy involves an advocacy group with the grassroots-sounding name the Clean and Safe Energy Coalition. At the center of the effort are former EPA [Enivronmental Protection Agency] chief Christine Todd Whitman and former Greenpeace co-founder turned corporate shill Patrick Moore. (Moore is also a huge champion of GMO [genetically modified organism] crops, which are notorious for impoverishing farmers in developing economies and using massive amounts of pesticides.) The industry also places ghostwritten op-eds under the bylines of scientists for hire.

All the major environmental groups oppose nuclear power. But the campaign is having some impact at the grassroots: the online environmental journal *Grist* found that 54 percent of its readers are ready to give atomic energy a second look; 59 percent of Treehugger.com readers feel the same way. In other

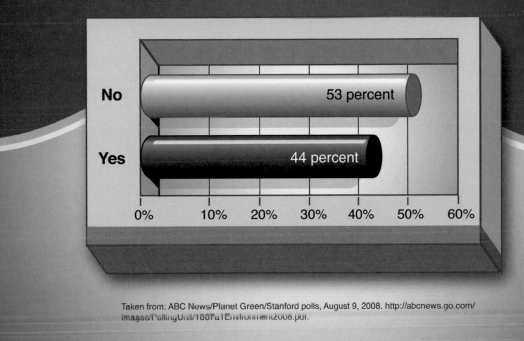

Most Americans Oppose Nuclear Power

Should the United States build more nuclear power plants?

No   53 percent

Yes   44 percent

0%   10%   20%   30%   40%   50%   60%

Taken from: ABC News/Planet Green/Stanford polls, August 9, 2008. http://abcnews.go.com/
images/PollingUnit/1007a1Environment2008.pdf.

words, people who understand climate change are feeling down-
right desperate. . . .

The Nuclear Waste Problem

Activists like [Diane] Sidebotham say the real issue is not how
to build more nukes but how to handle the old, decrepit plants
and their huge stockpiles of radioactive waste. Most of the
atomic plants in this country are reaching the end of their life
span; seventeen have been decommissioned. And increasingly
the question is what to do with the accumulated waste—the extremely radioactive spent fuel rods. This is dangerous stuff. If
exposed to air for more than six hours, spent fuel rods spontaneously combust, spewing highly poisonous radioactive isotopes
far and wide. This spent fuel will be hot for 10,000 years.

    Since 1978 the Energy Department has been studying Yucca
Mountain in Nevada as a possible permanent repository for

Depleted nuclear fuel rods are submerged in water in this spent fuel pool. Nuclear waste sites like this are scattered across the country because no central storage facility yet exists in the United States.

atomic waste. But intense opposition has held up those efforts. In the meantime, the partially burned uranium is stored at the old power plants, in pools of water called "spent fuel pools." Lying near great cities, on crucial river systems, in small rural towns, these pools are potentially a far greater risk than a reactor meltdown. Scenarios for how terrorists might attack and drain them range from driving a truck bomb to crashing an explosive-laden plane into them. . . .

Humanity's Faustian bargain with atomic power is a story still in its early stages. No one knows how long nuclear facilities will last or what will happen to them during future social upheavals—and there are bound to be a few of those during the next 10,000 years.

This much seems clear: a handful of firms might soak up huge federal subsidies and build one or two overpriced plants. While a new administration might tighten regulations, public safety will continue to be menaced by problems at new as well as older plants. But there will be no massive nuclear renaissance. Talk of such a renaissance, however, helps keep people distracted, their minds off the real project of developing wind, solar, geothermal and tidal kinetics to build a green power grid.

EIGHT

Hydrogen Fuel Cells Are a Good Alternative to Gasoline

Jerry Brown, Rinaldo Brutoco, and James Cusumano

Jerry Brown is a professor at Florida International University; Rinaldo Brutoco is the founder and president of the World Business Academy; and James Cusumano is a former director of research and development at Exxon. Together they coauthored the book *Freedom from Mid-East Oil*. In the following viewpoint the authors examine common objections to the use of hydrogen fuel cells in cars. They argue that these objections are based on a misunderstanding of hydrogen fuel cells and conclude that with the right strategy, hydrogen fuel cells could be the best alternative to gasoline engines in cars.

You may think hydrogen power is some futuristic fantasy, fit only for science-fiction writers. Or, at best, you might consider it a promising technology that won't be ready for prime time for another 40 to 50 years. If so, think again. In a special edition on "Best Inventions 2006," *Time* magazine praises the decision by Shanghai-based Horizon Fuel Cell Technologies "to design and market the H-racer, a 6-inch-long toy car that does what Detroit still can't. It runs on hydrogen extracted from plain tap water, using the solar-powered hydrogen station."

Jerry Brown, Rinaldo Brutoco, and James Cusumano, "Welcome to the Hydrogen Age," *Ode*, October 2007. www.odemagazine.com. © Ode Magazine USA, Inc. and Ode Luxembourg 2007. Reproduced by permission.

Hydrogen vehicles are not mere toys. More than 500 are on the road today. A BMW prototype with a hydrogen internal-combustion engine attained a top speed of 186 miles an hour. Mazda, Ford, Honda and GM are developing a variety of hydrogen-powered engines. Perhaps most exciting, Honda is now powering zero-emission vehicles with hydrogen derived from tap water in small stationary units that drivers can keep in their garages.

Hydrogen Fuel-Cell Cars Are Possible Today

We believe the rapid pace of invention, testing and commercialization of fuel-cell technologies is a strong sign that we are entering the early stages of a hydrogen revolution. Instead of waiting half a century as critics suggest, the large-scale production of hydrogen fuel-cell cars could begin very soon. We have come to a crossroads where a single, courageous decision by a few world leaders could launch a new era of progress. That decision is, of course, to shift from our dependence on environmentally damaging fossil fuels to plentiful, renewable and clean-burning hydrogen fuel.

Not everyone sees the bright future of the hydrogen age. Some well-informed energy experts contend hydrogen will be viable only after 20 to 30 years of development. The respected environmental think tank Worldwatch Institute cautions, "Despite recent public attention about the potential for a hydrogen economy, it could take decades to develop the infrastructure and vehicles required for a hydrogen-powered system." Joseph Romm, author of *The Hype About Hydrogen*, states that "hydrogen vehicles are unlikely to achieve even a 5 percent market share by 2030."

These predictions are needlessly pessimistic, based on common misconceptions about the cost, efficiency and technology of hydrogen. If we make hydrogen a national and international priority, as outlined below in a strategy for launching the hydrogen economy, we foresee the first affordable hydrogen fuel-cell cars coming to market starting between 2010 and 2012, and achieving 5 percent of the new car market share by 2020 or sooner.

A mock-up of a hydrogen fuel cell is shown here. The authors argue that the capability exists to begin mass production of hydrogen fuel-cell cars very soon.

Looking at Myths About Hydrogen

Let's examine the critics' misconceptions about hydrogen.

Myth No. 1: A hydrogen industry needs to be built from scratch. The production of hydrogen is already a large, mature industry, and the global hydrogen industry annually produces 50 million metric tons (50 billion kilograms) of hydrogen, worth about $150 billion. To put that into perspective, the current global output of pure hydrogen has the energy equivalence of 1.2 billion barrels of oil, or about a quarter of U.S. petroleum imports. The hydrogen industry is growing at 6 percent a year, thus doubling every 12 years. All this is happening without the incentives that would be provided by a growing fleet of hydrogen fuel-cell vehicles in need of fuel. If the hydrogen industry can expand so quickly "below the radar," it will have no problem expanding quickly enough to fuel the needs of hydrogen fuel-cell cars in the future.

Myth No. 2: Hydrogen is too dangerous for common use. This myth begins with the hydrogen-filled German zeppelin, the Hindenburg, which blew up at Lakehurst, New Jersey, in 1937. Recently that event was revisited in a detailed analysis by National Aeronautics and Space Administration (NASA) scientist Addison Bain. He found that it was not the hydrogen that originally combusted, but the dirigible's outer coating, a highly flammable material similar to that used in rocket propellants. In reality, the hydrogen industry has had an excellent safety record for decades. In 30 years, liquefied hydrogen shipments have logged 33 billion miles. During all this time, no product losses or fires were reported. Gasoline, our automotive fuel of choice, is 22 times more explosive and has a dismal safety record in comparison.

Hydrogen, while flammable, is generally more easily managed than hydrocarbon fuels. If hydrogen is ignited, it burns with a clear flame and only one-tenth the radiant heat of a hydrocarbon fire. The heat that is produced tends to dissipate much more rapidly than heat from gasoline or oil fires. The bottom line is that hydrogen-safety critics should turn their fire against gasoline, and agitate for the rapid adoption of hydrogen on safety grounds alone!

Myth No. 3: Hydrogen can't be distributed via existing pipelines. The transportation of hydrogen, one of the most frequently mentioned concerns of critics, is easily accomplished through pipelines. Creating a new pipeline network to move hydrogen is unnecessary; we can use the one already in existence. Some existing pipelines are already hydrogen-ready. The others can easily be modified with existing technologies by adding polymer-composite liners, similar to the process used to renovate old sewer pipes. Using existing pipelines creates no additional safety concerns. Already, hydrogen-refueling stations are appearing in California, Florida and British Columbia. Other regions are sure to follow.

Myth No. 4: There is no practical way to run cars on hydrogen. Hydrogen fuel cells have been used for space flights since 1965 and they were used in a passenger vehicle as early as 1966 (GM's Electrovan). Today, fuel-cell vehicles are undergoing rigorous testing and are far advanced. As of mid-2003, manufacturers had dozens of fuel-cell buses and upwards of 100 fuel-cell cars on the road. Fuel cells are being tested for military vehicles on land and sea; submarines have used them for years. Heavy trucks, which spend up to half their engine run time idling because they have no auxiliary power source, are also beginning to use fuel cells. FedEx and UPS plan to introduce fuel-cell trucks by next year [2008].

With such a massive wave of research and trial, fuel cells are sure to advance quickly, as each successful application benefits from its predecessors' experiences. As a whole, mass production will drive down the price of fuel cells.

Myth No. 5: Hydrogen is too expensive to compete with gasoline. Despite decades of U.S. policies favouring the use of petroleum, hydrogen technologies are already close to economic viability. When we consider system-wide life-cycle costs, hydrogen is already a desirable alternative to fossil fuel. The factor of greenhouse gas emissions makes hydrogen overwhelmingly preferable to gasoline. Even when hydrogen fuel is produced from natural gas, on a per-mile-driven basis, fuel-cell cars generate as little as 30 percent of the carbon dioxide produced by gasoline-powered cars. . . .

A Strategy for Hydrogen Cars

Given the urgency of the energy and climate crises, we urge development of a broad political consensus around a strategy for transitioning to a hydrogen economy. This strategy would apply regulatory, financial and other market-driven incentives while drawing on the best available technology and talent. Under the leadership of a non-partisan National Hydrogen Task Force, political leaders in the U.S. and elsewhere should convene the nation's leading hydrogen scientists, engineers and inventors, along with top environmental lawyers, finance experts and specialists in public/private enterprises. . . .

Work would also begin on a national hydrogen infrastructure, including production facilities, pipelines and fueling stations built in metropolitan areas. The ultimate goal by 2020 would be the broad transition to clean and green hydrogen generated from non-fossil fuels—wind, solar and possibly biological

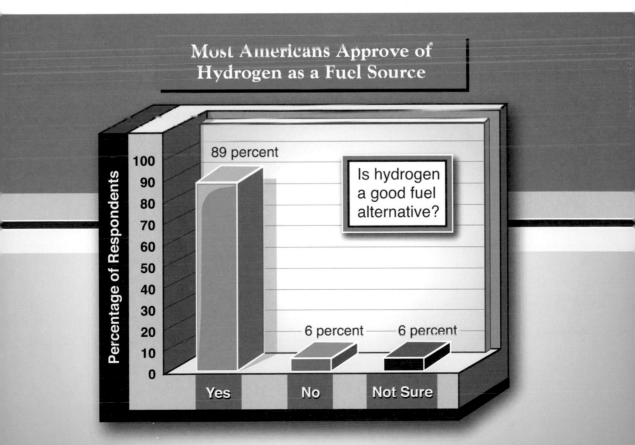

Most Americans Approve of Hydrogen as a Fuel Source

Is hydrogen a good fuel alternative?

89 percent

6 percent   6 percent

Percentage of Respondents

Yes   No   Not Sure

Figures are approximate.

Taken from: *Alternative Energy News*, February 2009.

systems—and minimum sales of a million hydrogen fuel-cell vehicles, equal to a 6 percent new-car market penetration. In parallel to these hydrogen milestones, the plan would require development of automobile engines that could function on a mix of plug-in technologies, renewable fuels such as ethanol or biodiesel and hydrogen fuel cells powered by electricity from the utility grid. . . .

The hydrogen economy is the only reliable long-term solution to the energy and climate crises confronting civilization. No other known technology option can safely produce clean energy to power transportation systems and other infrastructure at levels that can sustain current levels of global prosperity, let alone increase these levels to improve the lot of the world's poor. This great transition will be profitable and beneficial for all stakeholders. The hydrogen revolution is one of the greatest legacies our generation could pass on to our children and children's children.

Horace Mann, a pioneering 19th-century advocate of free public education in the U.S., said, "Be ashamed to die until you've won some great victory for humanity." All who join in this grand enterprise to bring about the birth of the hydrogen age will participate in one of humanity's greatest victories: the creation of a safe, clean and sustainable future.

NINE

Hydrogen Fuel Cells Are Not a Good Alternative to Gasoline

Charlie White

> Charlie White is the deputy editor of *Dvice*, a print and Web-based publication that focuses on new and emerging technologies. In the following viewpoint White argues that hydrogen fuel cells can never provide a realistic alternative to gasoline engines in cars. White discusses the problems with hydrogen fuel cell production and use, including the problems associated with creating and storing hydrogen as well as the high cost of manufacturing hydrogen fuel cells.

Who wouldn't like the idea of a fuel cell car running on clean, pure hydrogen, the universe's most plentiful element? Its byproduct is sparkling, drinkable water, with none of that pesky pollution spewing out the tailpipe. And then if there's any energy left over when you're done driving, why, you could use that car's fuel cell to power your house! We can get rid of gasoline! And fuel cells, hey, they use those in spacecraft, don't they? This is some modern stuff, and at first glance, hydrogen appears to be a viable solution to all our energy problems.

Well, think again. Hydrogen fuel cell cars are a dumb idea, and those who are pushing them are frauds. They want to advance their own agendas, and couldn't care less whether their cars are practical or not. They just want to make more money. In fact, their tired ideas for fuel cell vehicles have already been left in the dust by electric and hybrid vehicles, and there are a lot of good reasons why.

Hydrogen Cars Are Too Expensive

Fuel cell cars are available today. But wait, you can't really *buy* the Honda FCX Clarity—you must *rent* it for $600 a month. Why? Because if this wasn't a publicity stunt, you'd have to buy the FCX for its real cost. The car makers are secretive about how much it's costing to build these vehicles, but you can bet it's well into the hundreds of thousands of dollars apiece.

To give you an idea, mass producing a fuel cell–powered bus is going to cost $200,000 extra just for the engine, according to its designers at Caltech and the Jet Propulsion Laboratory. Pretty good, though, considering that just two years ago, the average cost of a fuel cell vehicle was a cool million dollars.

This huge cost issue is just the tip of this expensive iceberg. While some companies that are seeking funding for their fuel cell vehicle schemes say otherwise, the cars are notoriously impractical. I smell boondoggle.

Hydrogen Is Not a Fuel Alternative

No, hydrogen is not really a fuel, but an energy storage medium. It's more akin to a battery that soaks up energy when it's extracted from something else, and then delivers that energy when it's used. And, it takes a lot of energy to create that hydrogen. The energy must come from other sources, such as natural gas, or elaborate electrolysis using platinum membranes that separate the hydrogen and oxygen in water, using, um, electricity. What? Using electricity to make hydrogen that's then turned back into electricity? Yes, it's the laws of physics at work, where you have to put in energy to get some out. So you must use electricity or gas (or maybe solar energy) to make this stuff. So yeah, it works like a battery, except a whole lot more expensive. Why not just charge up an electric car instead?

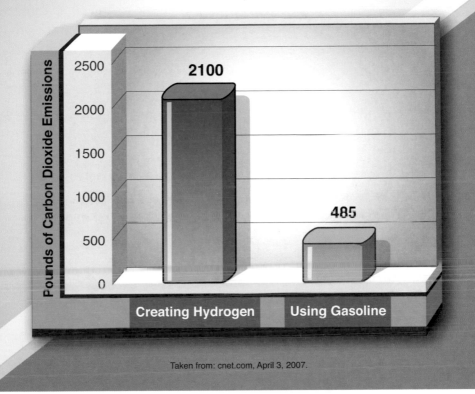

Creating Hydrogen Produces More Carbon Emissions than Using Gasoline

Creating enough hydrogen to drive a car 1,000 miles results in carbon emissions four times greater than using gasoline to drive the same car 1,000 miles.

Pounds of Carbon Dioxide Emissions

2500
2000
1500
1000
500
0

2100

485

Creating Hydrogen | Using Gasoline

Taken from: cnet.com, April 3, 2007.

Hydrogen Is Difficult to Handle

No, there's no such thing as a hydrogen well. It doesn't just gather in one place like oil or natural gas does, but quickly dissipates into the atmosphere because of its simple atomic structure. Because of that number-one position on the periodic table, hydrogen is difficult to store and corrodes pipes. It's a clever escape artist, and can even slip between the molecules of steel or aluminum containers. So hydrogen can't be stored long-term—it must be created on the spot by stripping it from other molecules.

These fuel cell cars need four times the volume to store an amount of energy equal to that of gasoline. Even though the energy-generating equivalent of hydrogen is lighter than its gasoline counterpart, you need a 60 gallon tank to store the same amount of energy that's in 15 gallons of gasoline. These cars won't go far before it's time for more hydrogen.

The oil companies would like to provide the infrastructure for such a "hydrogen economy." The oil companies say to you, "No, don't use electricity from your house to charge up that electric vehicle—depend on the oil company's filling stations to get where you want to go, as you've always done."

Good luck with that, though, because so far there's just one retail hydrogen station in the U.S. (run by, you guessed it, an oil company), far short of the thousands needed to make this hydrogen economy anything more than a pipe dream. The other

The author argues that the support of former president George W. Bush (left) for hydrogen cars is tied to the oil industry's desire to control the "hydrogen economy."

experimental stations are nothing but showboat propaganda fronts that expend far more energy than they create. Anyway, the oil companies would be happy to invest in that costly infrastructure, because they know they'll get their money back. But it'll be coming out of your hide, just like it always has.

Hydrogen Fuel Cells Are a Bad Idea

There are a variety of impractical ideas for using hydrogen to propel cars, but they're years—and maybe even decades—from being cost-effective. Most of these schemes seem to suspiciously somehow involve the oil companies keeping their greedy paws in the "hydrogen economy." To give you an idea, one great proponent of the "hydrogen economy" is energy expert, former oilman, [former U.S. president] and conservation guru George W. Bush.

We're all for innovation, but the fantasy of cost-effective hydrogen fuel cell vehicles is just a distraction from the real work that needs to be done: perfecting electric and hybrid natural gas/electric vehicles, charged by electricity generated by clean and renewable nuclear, solar, wind, geothermal and hydroelectric power. These technologies are here now, and the associated batteries are getting more efficient at a rate that's significantly faster than the snail's pace of impractical fuel cell technology. Maybe someday hydrogen fuel cells will be practical for personal vehicles, but not today, and not for a long time to come. Don't be fooled by the self-serving frauds that keep trying to tell you otherwise.

TEN

Solar Power Is a Good Alternative for Making Electricity

Bruce Allen

Bruce Allen is an independent journalist whose writing focuses on solar power, electric vehicles, and national energy policy. He is a physicist and inventor specializing in spacecraft technology development. In the following viewpoint Allen looks at the growth of the solar power industry in recent years. He discusses new technology used to collect solar energy and methods being developed to generate, store, and distribute electricity made from solar power. Allen argues that solar power is the cleanest and most effective alternative method for creating electricity.

Over the next 10 years, we will likely see the U.S. reach a solar tipping point.

Solar energy has always been one of the cleanest and longest lasting of all energy sources. Soon, it may be one of the cheapest. The January [2008] *Scientific American* article, "A Solar Grand Plan" provides a glimpse of the possibilities of large-scale solar farms driving America's energy future. (Currently, solar provides less than 0.01 percent of the electricity the U.S. uses.)

Is there a more practical and compelling solution that lets us reach a tipping point more quickly?

Bruce Allen, "Reaching the Solar Tipping Point," *Miller-McCune*, September 4, 2008. http:// miller-mccune.com. © 2008 Miller-McCune Inc. Reproduced by permission.

The "Solar Grand Plan" envisions thin-film cadmium telluride photovoltaics [systems that convert light to electricity], currently 11 percent efficient, supplemented with solar thermal farms, blanketing vast stretches of our Southwestern deserts and pumping electricity into a more efficient national high voltage, direct-current (HVDC) grid. Nighttime and cloudy-weather worries would be eased by holding electricity via compressed air storage in caverns to drive generators.

But compressed air storage is only about 75 percent efficient, and there are concerns about production scalability for the thousands of square miles of panels featuring tellurium, one of the rarest metallic elements on Earth.

Solar Farms Are Effective

A more efficient large-scale solar energy solution for the United States may be based on desert solar thermal farms with overnight heat storage and HVDC transmission. Thermal heat storage is up to 95 percent efficient and can cost-effectively convert stored heat into electricity at night and in cloudy weather for up to 16 hours.

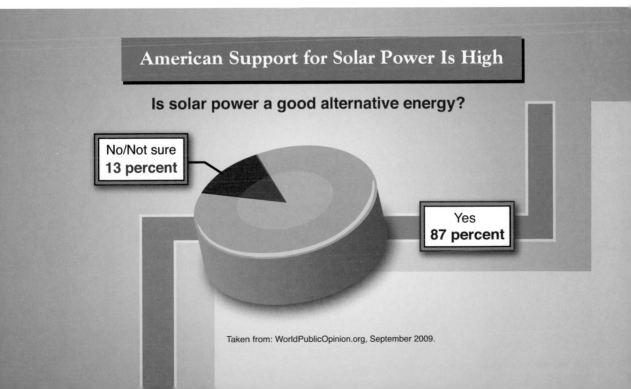

American Support for Solar Power Is High

Is solar power a good alternative energy?

No/Not sure
13 percent

Yes
87 percent

Taken from: WorldPublicOpinion.org, September 2009.

Solar trough farms are the leading solar thermal commercial technology, with solar-concentrating towers gaining commercial traction.

Solar thermal farms would be supplemented with crystalline and thin-film photovoltaic arrays, rooftop and building-integrated photovoltaics (BIPV) capturing the best features of centralized and distributed generation.

Generating electricity that can't be delivered nationally, as renewable energy partisans are discovering, is spurring the co-development of HVDC to supersede America's antiquated power grid, which was not built with routine transcontinental movement in mind. One example of the ability of HVDC to economically deliver long-distance electricity is the giant Itaipu Dam Transmission Project in Brazil, providing 6,300 megawatts to São Paulo, South America's largest city, over a distance of 800 km (about 500 miles) since 1991.

The performance of modern solar thermal trough systems is highly refined compared with previous generations. They offer massive cost-effective scale with virtually no manufacturing bottlenecks, and their new reflector and heat pipe designs have reduced costs, increased durability and produce electricity more efficiently.

The Cost of Solar Farms

Costs of newer solar thermal farms are approaching $2.75 per kilowatt, significantly less than current photovoltaic-installed costs. The National Renewable Energy Laboratory estimates that these systems, with energy storage, can achieve a cost of 7 cents per kilowatt-hour within 10 years. (The average price of electricity nationally was 9.09 cents per kilowatt-hour in March [2008].)

Today's leading solar thermal manufacturers, including Ausra, Acciona, Abengoa and Solel, are achieving in excess of 17 percent total conversion efficiency of sunlight to electricity and have the capacity to build solar thermal farms measured in square miles per year. In the near future, solar thermal manufactures will have factory capacity for solar farms covering tens to hundreds of square miles per year.

How much desert is required to power the U.S. with solar thermal farms supplemented with photovoltaics?

A modern "compact linear fresnel reflector" thermal farm requires about 2.5 acres per megawatt, about half the area required by previous solar trough or thin-film photovoltaic farms. One next-generation solar farm is the 177-megawatt Ausra plant currently being permitted in California and expected to be online in 2010.

A solar thermal study co-authored by David Mills, the chairman of Ausra, estimated the total area of solar thermal farms needed to have supplied more than 90 percent of U.S. electricity needs in 2006 to be 13,000 square miles (about the size of two Hawaiis). Dividing the land area between California, Nevada, Arizona, New Mexico, Southern Utah and West Texas would limit the area covered to about 2,000 square miles in each state.

New Efficiencies in Solar Technology

Photovoltaics on rooftops and integrated into buildings reduce the area required for solar thermal farms and allow more energy to be directed to overnight and cloudy weather backup heat storage.

On a more human scale, the typical U.S. household uses 30 kilowatt-hours per day, equivalent to approximately 250 square feet of 19-percent efficient rooftop panels on a cloudless day.

Also offering a reduction in the solar footprint are advances in photovoltaic technology. For example, industry leader Sunpower's silicon solar cell and panel efficiencies now exceed 22 percent and 19 percent respectively.

The estimate from Mills included electricity demand for transportation if all car and truck transportation needs had been met by electric vehicles. The power of combining electric vehicles and solar electricity is that electric vehicles are about 85 percent efficient at converting electricity to motion; internal combustion vehicles are around 17 to 25 percent efficient. Manufacturing aside, electric vehicles powered by solar electricity are pollution and carbon-emission free, unlike gas-, diesel- and ethanol-fueled vehicles.

Thomas Warner, chief executive officer of the SunPower Corporation, displays his company's new silicon solar cell, which substantially reduces the solar footprint required to produce energy.

One acre of solar thermal farmland can provide the same useful electric vehicle transportation energy per year as 100 acres of switch grass converted to cellulosic ethanol.

The Growth of Solar Power

The dual growth of large-scale solar thermal farms and photovoltaics is on track to become the largest single source of newly installed electric-generating capacity in the U.S. in the next 10 years—the solar tipping point.

Solar photovoltaic capacity growth is expected to continue at more than 50 percent per year for the next five years. American chemical giant DuPont reiterated that statistic on Sept. 2 [2008] as it estimated its own sales into the photovoltaic industry would exceed $1 billion within five years.

Meanwhile, solar thermal capacity and installations are growing rapidly. Ausra's new automated Las Vegas solar thermal factory capacity is more than 700 megawatts per year.

Because solar thermal farm materials are based on abundant industrial materials including steel, glass and conventional electrical generating turbines, solar thermal factories can scale to beyond gigawatt capacity in only a few more years. The primary limitations are continuing incremental cost reductions, land-use permitting timelines and regional and national electric-grid-expansion agreements.

While solar thermal farms can also begin supplying nighttime and backup storage capacity, retaining existing natural gas electric power plants and integrating natural gas co-generation at solar thermal farms also can provide responsive cloudy weather capacity. Additional but less efficient cloudy weather backup power could be provided by hydrogen electrolysis—creating hydrogen as a fuel from water—or compressed air storage.

The scale of photovoltaic capacity expansion is also accelerating. Pacific Gas and Electric in August signed contracts for the world's two largest photovoltaic farms comprising 800 MW covering 12.4 square miles in a remote valley in Central California. Optisolar will build a 550 MW solar farm using thin-film silicon photovoltaic panels, and SunPower will build a 250 MW plant using its high-efficiency crystalline-silicon PV panels.

State and local governments are also shortening the time it will take to reach the solar tipping point. California approved a law in July that allows cities and counties to provide low-interest energy loans, including for residential solar installations, with payments added to property tax bills over 20 years.

Clean solar energy may be our manifest destiny.

ELEVEN

Solar Power Is Not a Good Alternative for Making Electricity

Otis A. Glazebrook IV

Otis A. Glazebrook IV is a frequent contributor to *American Thinker*. In the following viewpoint Glazebrook argues that although electricity generated from solar power is clean, the process used to manufacture solar panels is not. Glazebrook provides details on a number of the toxic chemicals that are involved in the solar panel manufacturing and disposal processes, and he compares these to the by-products of burning coal. He concludes that because of the toxic solar panel manufacturing process, solar power is not an acceptable substitute for the use of coal.

You think solar electrical generation is going to save you or the Planet? Think again.

While it is true that photovoltaic [systems that convert light into electricity] solar panels do not pollute while they are producing electricity—what about the manufacturing process? What happens when these panels reach the end of their projected lifecycle in twenty-five years? (This is, by the way, an optimistic view of their useful life.) Those questions are addressed in a study by the watchdog group Silicon Valley Toxics Coalition.

"Green Power" is being hyped as the "Safe Solution." It is anything but safe—when all factors are considered.

Toxic Byproducts of Solar Panel Manufacturing

Here is a partial list (eight of fifty) of chemicals associated with solar photovoltaic (PV) manufacturing and disposal:

Arsenic (As) can be released from the decomposition of discarded GaAs [gallium arsenide] solar PV cells. Inhalation of high levels of arsenic causes throat soreness, lung irritation, increased lung cancer risk, nausea and vomiting, decreased production of red and white blood cells, abnormal heart rhythm, damage to blood vessels, and "pins and needles" sensations in hands and feet. Ingesting or breathing low levels of inorganic arsenic for an extended period causes skin darkening, and small "corns" or "warts" appear on the palms, soles, and torso. Skin contact may cause redness and swelling. Ingestion can increase skin, liver, bladder, and lung cancer risks. Ingesting very high levels can result in death.

Cadmium (Cd) is a byproduct of zinc, lead, or copper mining. Workers can be exposed through cadmium smelting and refining or through the air in workplaces that make Cd-based semiconductors. Acute symptoms vary depending on the specific cadmium compound, but can include pulmonary edema, cough, chest tightening, headache, chills, muscle aches, nausea, vomiting, and diarrhea. Cd is chronically toxic to the respiratory system, kidneys, prostate, and blood and can cause prostate and lung cancer. NIOSH [National Institute for Occupational Safety and Health] considers cadmium dust and vapors as carcinogens. California has also determined (under AB 1807 and Proposition 65) that cadmium and cadmium compounds are carcinogens.

Chromium VI (Cr VI) is used in PV modules for chrome-plated hardware such as screws and frames. High levels of chromium have provoked asthma attacks, and long-term exposure is associated with lung cancer. Handling liquids or solids containing Cr VI can cause skin ulcers. Swallowing large amounts will cause upset stomach, ulcers, convulsions, kidney

Solar Panel Manufacturing Is Toxic

About 50 percent of the toxic material used to make solar panels is released into the air or water during the manufacturing process. Workers are also exposed to toxic materials.

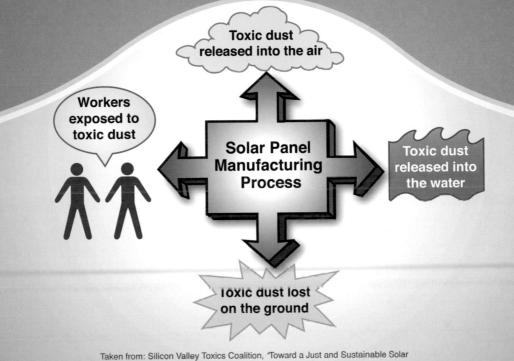

Taken from: Silicon Valley Toxics Coalition, "Toward a Just and Sustainable Solar Energy Industry," January 14, 2009.

and liver damage, and even death. The EPA [Environmental Protection Agency] classifies Cr VI as a known human carcinogen.

Hexafluoroethane (C_2F_6) is used to etch semiconductors. It is an asphyxiant and in high concentrations may cause dizziness, nausea, vomiting, disorientation, confusion, loss of coordination, and narcosis. Very high concentrations may cause suffocation. Liquid hexafluoroethane may cause frostbite. Harmful amounts may be absorbed if skin contact is prolonged or widespread. It is listed as a potent greenhouse gas by the IPCC [Intergovernmental Panel on Climate Change].

Nitrogen trifluoride (NF_3) is used to clean reactors and etch polysilicon semiconductors. It emits toxic fumes when burned or reacted and can cause asphyxiation. The IPCC considers NF_3 a significant greenhouse gas, making fugitive emission control very important.

Selenium (Se) is found in CIS/CIGS [semiconductor materials used in thin-film solar cells] as an alloy of diselenide. Short-term exposure to high concentrations of selenium may cause nausea, vomiting, and diarrhea. Chronic exposure to high concentrations of selenium compounds can produce a disease called selenosis. Major signs of selenosis are hair loss, nail brittleness, and neurological abnormalities (such as numbness and other odd sensations in the extremities). Brief exposures to high levels of Se can result in respiratory tract irritation, bronchitis, difficulty breathing, and stomach pains.

Silane (SiH$_4$) gas is used to apply silicon thin films and make silicon crystal semiconductors. Major health hazards include respiratory tract, skin, and eye irritation. Silane gas is extremely explosive. At room temperature, silane is pyrophoric—it spontaneously combusts in air without external ignition.

Tetrabromo bisphenol A (TBBPA) is a reactive brominated flame retardant used in the printed wiring boards of more than 90 percent of electrical and electronic products. The main use of TBBPA in solar PV is in inverters. Occupational exposure may occur from contact during production or through dust inhalation. Recent concerns focus on TBBPA as an endocrine disruptor; it is similar to bisphenol A, a known estrogen mimic. TBBPA also bioaccumulates in organisms.

Comparing Byproducts of Coal Use

Compare this with the byproducts of coal combustion from the Coal Utilization Byproduct Research:

Each year, the U.S. electric utility industry generates about 100 million tons of coal combustion byproducts. Just over half of this amount is fly ash (a talcum-like solid in the flue gas from a coal-fired boiler), approximately one-fourth is sludge from wet flue gas scrubbers, another 16 percent is boiler ash (a heavier, coarser solid removed from the bottom of a boiler), and about 7 percent is boiler slag (a hard, glassy material made from boiler ash that has been melted by the heat of the combustor).

Currently only about a third of this coal ash and just over one fourth of the scrubber waste is recycled in commercially beneficial uses. The largest amount is fly ash that is typically used as a Portland cement replacement in concrete and concrete products. The remainder, more than 70 million tons a year, is disposed of in impoundments and landfills.

Many experts believe the coal combustion byproducts represent a vastly underused resource. Combustion byproducts can

Fly ash, one of the waste products from coal combustion, is recycled for use as a replacement for cement in the manufacture of concrete.

strengthen construction materials and reduce overall product costs. The gypsum-rich byproducts of flue gas scrubbers can provide plants with nutrients and enhance depleted soils in various agricultural applications. Coal combustion byproducts can be used to immobilize hazardous wastes for safer disposal.

Greater use of coal combustion byproducts can also help reduce concerns over greenhouse gases. Using fly ash for cement making, for example, reduces the need for limestone calcination, a process that requires a large amount of heat typically provided by burning fossil fuels. For every ton of fly ash used in concrete, approximately 0.8 tons of carbon dioxide would be prevented from being released into the atmosphere.

Notice how the "Green Solutions" always seem to create more problems and pollution than they could ever be expected to solve?

TWELVE

Wind Power Is a Good Alternative for Making Electricity

Charles Komanoff

Charles Komanoff is an environmental activist and economic policy analyst who advocates for energy efficiency, bicycle transportation, and urban revitalization. He is the author of the book *Power Plant Cost Escalation*. In the following viewpoint Komanoff examines the pros and cons of wind power. He acknowledges the challenges associated with the installation and use of large wind turbines and discusses the efficiency and reliability of wind power. Considering the drawbacks and benefits of wind power, Komanoff concludes that it is a good way to generate electricity.

Although automobiles, with their appetite for petroleum, may seem like the main culprit in causing global warming, the number one climate change agent in the U.S. is actually electricity. The most recent inventory of U.S. greenhouse gases found that power generation was responsible for a whopping 38 percent of carbon dioxide [CO_2] emissions. Yet the electricity sector may also be the least complicated to make carbon free. Approximately three-fourths of U.S. electricity is generated by burning coal, oil, or natural gas. Accordingly, switching that same portion of U.S. electricity generation to nonpolluting sources such as wind turbines, while simultaneously ensuring that our ever-expanding arrays of lights, computers, and appliances are increasingly energy efficient, would eliminate 38 percent of the country's CO_2 emissions and bring us halfway to the goal of cutting emissions by 75 percent.

Switching to Wind Power

To achieve that power switch entirely through wind power, I calculate, would require 400,000 windmills rated at 2.5 megawatts each. To be sure, this is a hypothetical figure, since it ignores such real-world issues as limits on power transmission and the intermittency of wind, but it's a useful benchmark just the same.

What would that entail?

To begin, I want to be clear that the turbines I'm talking about are huge, with blades up to 165 feet long mounted on towers rising several hundred feet. Household wind machines like the 100-foot-high Bergey 10-kilowatt BWC Excel with 11-foot blades, the mainstay of the residential and small business wind turbine market, may embody democratic self-reliance and other "small is beautiful" virtues, but we can't look to them to make a real dent in the big energy picture. What dictates the supersizing of windmills are two basic laws of wind physics: a wind turbine's energy potential is proportional to the square of the length of the blades, and to the cube of the speed at which the blades spin. I'll spare you the math, but the difference in blade lengths, the greater wind speeds higher off the ground, and the sophisticated controls available on industrial-scale turbines all add up to a market-clinching five-hundred-fold advantage in electricity output for a giant General Electric or Vestas wind machine.

How much land do the industrial turbines require? The answer turns on what "require" means. An industry rule of thumb is that to maintain adequate exposure to the wind, each big turbine needs space around it of about 60 acres. Since 640 acres make a square mile, those 400,000 turbines would need 37,500 square miles, or roughly all the land in Indiana or Maine.

On the other hand, the land actually occupied by the turbines —their "footprint"—would be far, far smaller. For example, each 3.6-megawatt Cape Wind turbine proposed for Nantucket Sound will rest on a platform roughly 22 feet in diameter, implying a surface area of 380 square feet—the size of a typical one-bedroom apartment in New York City. Scaling that up by 400,000 suggests that just six square miles of land—less than the area of a single big Wyoming strip mine—could house the bases for all of the windmills needed to banish coal, oil, and gas from the U.S. electricity sector.

The Pros and Cons of Wind Power

Of course, erecting and maintaining wind turbines can also necessitate clearing land: ridgeline installations often require a fair amount of deforestation, and then there's the associated clearing for access roads, maintenance facilities, and the like. But there are also now a great many turbines situated on farmland, where the fields around their bases are still actively farmed.

Depending, then, on both the particular terrain and how the question is understood, the land area said to be needed for wind power can vary across almost four orders of magnitude. Similar divergences of opinion are heard about every other aspect of wind power, too. Big wind farms kill thousands of birds and bats—or hardly any, in comparison to avian mortality from other tall structures such as skyscrapers. Industrial wind machines are soft as a whisper from a thousand feet away, and even up close their sound level would rate as "quiet" on standard noise charts—or they can sound like "a grinding noise" or "the shrieking sound of a wild animal," according to one unhappy neighbor of an upstate New York wind farm. Wind power developers are skimming millions via subsidies, state-mandated quotas, and "green power" scams—or are boldly risking their own capital to strike a blow for clean energy against the fossil fuel Goliath.

Some of the bad press is warranted. The first giant wind farm, comprising six thousand small, fast-spinning turbines placed directly in northern California's principal raptor flyway,

Altamont Pass, in the early 1980s rightly inspired the epithet "Cuisinarts for birds." The longer blades on newer turbines rotate more slowly and thus kill far fewer birds, but bat kills are being reported at wind farms in the Appalachian Mountains; as many as two thousand bats were hacked to death at one forty-four-turbine installation in West Virginia. And as with any machine, some of the nearly ten thousand industrial-grade windmills now operating in the U.S. may groan or shriek when

Because they are designed with longer blades that rotate more slowly than those of earlier models, these power-generating windmills in California kill fewer birds.

something goes wrong. (From my own observations at a wind farm in upstate New York, backed up by readings from my sound meter, the turbines weren't terribly noisy even from up close and were barely audible from a thousand feet away.) Moreover, wind power does benefit from a handsome federal subsidy; indeed, uncertainty over renewal of the "production tax credit" worth 1.9 cents per kilowatt-hour nearly brought wind power development to a standstill a few years ago.

At the same time, however, there is an apocalyptic quality to much anti-wind advocacy that seems wildly disproportionate to the actual harm, particularly in the overall context of not just other sources of energy but modern industry in general. New York State opponents of wind farms call their website "Save Upstate New York," as if ecological or other damage from wind turbines might administer the coup de grâce to the state's rural provinces that decades of industrialization and pollution, followed by outsourcing, have not. In neighboring Massachusetts, a group called Green Berkshires argues that wind turbines "are enormously destructive to the environment," but does not perform the obvious comparison to the destructiveness of fossil fuel–based power. Although the intensely controversial Cape Wind project "poses an imminent threat to navigation and raises many serious maritime safety issues," according to the anti-wind Alliance to Protect Nantucket Sound, the alliance was strangely silent when an oil barge bound for the region's electric power plant spilled ninety-eight thousand gallons of its deadly, gluey cargo into Buzzards Bay [in 2008].

The Reliability of Wind Power

Of course rhetoric is standard fare in advocacy, particularly the environmental variety with its salvationist mentality—environmentalists always like to feel they are "saving" this valley or that species. It all comes down to a question of what we're saving, and for whom. You can spend hours sifting through the anti-wind websites and find no mention at all of the climate crisis, let alone wind power's potential to help avert it.

In fact, many wind power opponents deny that wind power displaces much, if any, fossil fuel burning. Green Berkshires insists, for example, that "global warming [and] dependence on fossil fuels . . . will not be ameliorated one whit by the construction of these turbines on our mountains."

This notion is mistaken. It is true that since wind is variable, individual wind turbines can't be counted on to produce on demand, so the power grid can't necessarily retire fossil fuel generators at the same rate as it takes on windmills. The coal- and oil-fired generators will still need to be there, waiting for a windless day. But when the wind blows, those generators can spin down. That's how the grid works: it allocates electrons. Supply more electrons from one source, and other sources can supply fewer. And since system operators program the grid to draw from the lowest-cost generators first, and wind power's "fuel," moving air, is free, wind-generated electrons are given priority. It follows that more electrons from wind power mean proportionately fewer from fossil fuel burning.

What about the need to keep a few power stations burning fuel so they can instantaneously ramp up and counterbalance fluctuations in wind energy output? The grid requires this ballast, known as spinning reserve, in any event both because demand is always changing and because power plants of any type are subject to unforeseen breakdowns. The additional variability due to wind generation is slight—wind speeds don't suddenly drop from strong to calm, at least not for every turbine in a wind farm and certainly not for every wind farm on the grid. The clear verdict of the engineers responsible for grid reliability—a most conservative lot—is that the current level of wind power development will not require additional spinning reserve, while even much larger supplies of wind-generated electricity could be accommodated through a combination of energy storage technologies and improved models for predicting wind speeds.

With very few exceptions, then, wind output can be counted on to displace fossil fuel burning one for one. No less than other nonpolluting technologies like bicycles or photovoltaic solar cells, wind power is truly an anti-fossil fuel. . . .

The Cost of Wind Power

Part of the problem with wind power, I suspect, is that it's hard to weigh the effects of any one wind farm against the greater problem of climate change. It's much easier to comprehend the immediate impact of wind farm development than the less tangible losses from a warming Earth. And so the sacrifice is difficult, and it becomes progressively harder as rising affluence brings ever more profligate uses of energy.

Picture this: Swallowing hard, with deep regret for the change in a beloved landscape formerly unmarked in any obvious way by humankind, you've just cast the deciding affirmative vote to permit a wind farm on the hills outside your town. On the way home you see a new Hummer in your neighbor's driveway. How do you not feel like a self-sacrificing sucker?

Intruding the unmistakable human hand on any landscape for wind power is, of course, a loss in local terms, and no small one, particularly if the site is a verdant ridgeline. Uplands are not just visible markers of place but fragile environments, and the inevitable access roads for erecting and serving the turbines can be damaging ecologically as well as symbolically. In contrast, few if any benefits of the wind farm will be felt by you in a tangible way. If the thousands of tons of coal a year that your wind farm will replace were being mined now, a mile from your house, it might be a little easier to take. Unfortunately, our society rarely works that way. The bread you cast upon the waters with your vote will not come back to you in any obvious way—it will be eaten in Wyoming, or Appalachia. And you may just have to mutter an oath about the Hummer and use your moral imagination to console yourself about the ridge. . . .

Throughout his illustrious career, wilderness champion David Brower called upon Americans "to determine that an untrammeled wildness shall remain here to testify that this generation had love for the next." Now that all wild things and all places are threatened by global warming, that task is more complex.

Could a windmill's ability to "derive maximum benefit out of the site-specific gift nature is providing—wind and open

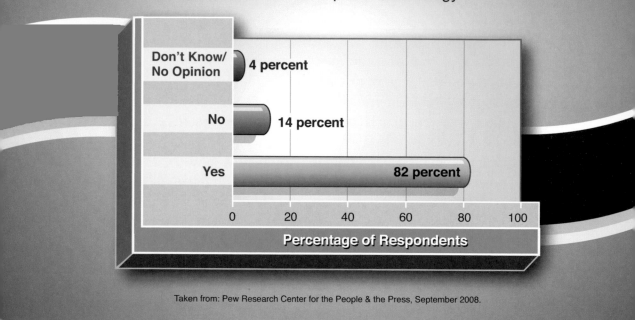

Americans Support More Research on Wind Power

Should the government increase funding for research on wind power technology?

Don't Know/ No Opinion — 4 percent

No — 14 percent

Yes — 82 percent

0   20   40   60   80   100

Percentage of Respondents

Taken from: Pew Research Center for the People & the Press, September 2008.

space," in the words of aesthetician Yuriko Saito, help Americans bridge the divide between pristine landscapes and sustainable ones? Could windmills help Americans subscribe to the "higher order of beauty" that environmental educator David Orr defines as something that "causes no ugliness somewhere else or at some later time"? Could acceptance of wind farms be our generation's way of avowing our love for the next?

I believe so. Or want to.

THIRTEEN

Wind Power Is Not a Good Alternative for Making Electricity

Glenn Schleede

Glenn Schleede is an expert on wind energy, energy markets, and energy policy analysis. He is a frequent contributor to the energy-related blog MasterResource and has published many papers and reports on energy-related topics. In the following viewpoint Schleede argues that government leaders and the media have misled the public about the effectiveness of wind power. He discusses common, incorrect assumptions about wind power and states that current statistics related to wind power are false. Schleede concludes that wind power is not a reliable alternative method of generating electricity.

People who use the phrase "homes served" to describe the potential output from one or more wind turbines either do not understand the facts about wind turbines, believe false claims put forth by the wind industry, or are trying to mislead their reader or listener. False statements about "homes served" by wind developers and their lobbyists are bad enough, but it is discouraging to hear politicians, reporters, and others adopt and regurgitate them.

The concept of "homes served" has long been used in the electric industry as a way of giving some idea of the amount of

Glenn Schleede, "Beware Windpower's 'Homes Served' Claims," MasterResource, February 4, 2009. http://masterresource.org. Reproduced by permission of the author.

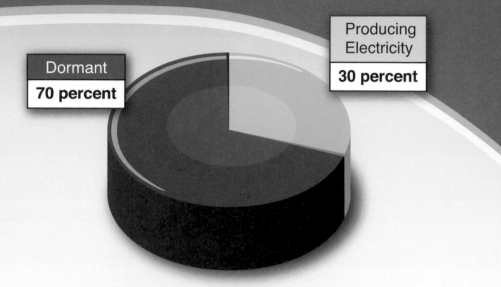

Wind Energy Is Unreliable

This chart shows the average percentage of time that wind turbines are active.

Producing Electricity

30 percent

Dormant

70 percent

Taken from: LiveScience.com, "5 Myths About Wind Energy," September 24, 2008.

electricity that would be produced by a proposed generating plant without using such terms as megawatt- or kilowatt-hours, which mean little to most people. The concept is always misleading since residential users of electricity (i.e., "homes served") account for only 37% of all U.S. electricity use.

Claims about "homes served" by a proposed "wind farm" or other generating unit are usually based on a three-step calculation:

- Start with an assumption (i.e., a guess) about the amount of electricity that would be *produced* annually by a "wind farm" or other generating unit, in kilowatt-hours (kWh) or megawatt-hours (MWh).
- Employ an estimate (in kWh) of the amount of electricity used annually by an average residential customer in the area or state where their "wind farm" is located.
- Divide the assumed annual production of electricity by the estimated annual average residential electricity use.

Although misleading, the concept of "homes served" has some validity when used to describe the *output from a reliable, "dispatchable" electric generating unit,* that is, one that can be called upon to produce electricity whenever it is needed. Such generating units are the ones that are counted on by the electric industry to provide a reliable supply of electricity for customers every day, at all hours of the day, year round.

Wind Power Is Not a Reliable Source of Electricity

Using "homes served" when talking about wind turbines and "wind farms" is both false and misleading for several reasons.

1. *NO homes are really served by wind.* No homes are served by wind energy because wind turbines produce electricity only when wind speeds are in the right speed range (see below). Homes using electricity from wind must always have some reliable energy source immediately available to provide electricity when there is insufficient wind unless the residents are content to have electricity only when the wind is blowing in the right speed range—a condition that few in America are willing to tolerate.

2. *Electricity from wind turbines is inherently intermittent, volatile, and unreliable.* Wind turbines produce electricity only when the wind is blowing within the right speed range. Wind turbines typically start producing electricity at about 6 mph, reach rated capacity at about 32 mph, and cut out at about 56 mph. Unless a home owner has an expensive battery storage system, such volatile and unreliable output wouldn't be suitable for lights, heating, computers, appliances, or many other purposes.

3. *Electricity from "wind farms" is seldom available when most needed by home users.* Again, the output of wind turbines is dependent on wind conditions. Depending on the specific area, winds tend to be strongest at night in cold months. However, electricity demand in most areas of the United States is heavily concentrated during daytime and early evening hours. Even worse, wind turbines cannot be counted on to produce at the time of peak electricity demand, which often occurs in late afternoon on hot weekdays in July and August. At the time of

The author strongly disagrees with wind power proponents who contend that wind power reduces U.S. reliance on foreign oil, is inexpensive, and is ecologically beneficial.

peak electricity demand, wind turbine output may be in the range of 0% to 5% of rated capacity.

4. *The electricity produced by wind turbines is low in value compared to electricity from reliable generating units.* That's because it is inherently intermittent, volatile, unreliable, and not available when most needed—as described in points 2 and 3 above.

5. *Not all the electricity produced by a wind turbine actually reaches customers or serves a useful purpose.* Some electricity is lost as it is moved over transmission and distribution lines that carry the electricity from generating units to homes, offices, stores, factories and other users. The amount of electricity that is lost depends on the distance and the condition of lines and

transformers. These "line losses" are a significant issue for wind energy because huge, obtrusive wind turbines (often 40+ stories tall) and "wind farms" are not welcome near metropolitan areas that account for most electricity demand. Therefore, they are often located at some distance from the areas where their electricity is needed and so require expensive transmission-line capacity, which they use inefficiently. (Ironically, the lucrative federal tax credits provided to "wind farm" owners are based on electricity *produced*, not the lesser amount that actually reaches customers and serves a useful purpose.)

6. *Claims of "homes served" by wind energy are additionally misleading because of the high true cost of electricity from wind turbines.* Claims that the cost of electricity from wind turbines is "competitive" with the cost of electricity from traditional sources are false. Such claims typically do not include the cost of (a) the huge federal and state tax breaks available to "wind farm" owners, or (b) the cost of providing the generating capacity and generation that must always be immediately available to "back up" intermittent, unreliable wind turbine output and keep electric grids reliable and in balance.

Statistics About Wind Energy Are Unreliable

Any use of the "homes served" assertion in connection with a "wind farm" should be challenged, whether the assertion is from a wind industry lobbyist, other wind energy advocate, political leader, other government official, or reporter. They should be required to explain each of their assumptions and calculations, and admit that industrial scale wind turbines are useless unless reliable generating units are immediately available to supply electricity when wind is not strong enough to produce significant electricity. Almost certainly, their assertions will be false.

As explained above, wind industry developers, promoters, and lobbyists—and politicians and reporters—should never use the false and misleading "homes served" metric. In theory, they could justify an assertion that the estimated amount of electricity produced by a "wind farm"—*once discounted for line losses which are likely to be in the range of 5% to 10%*—may be roughly equal to the amount of electricity used annually by X homes—after doing a calculation such as that outlined earlier. However, as indicated above, even this assertion would be misleading because it ignores the fact that the output from wind turbines is intermittent, volatile, unreliable, and unlikely to be available when electricity is most needed.

Statistics About Wind Energy Are Usually False

As shown above, "homes served" is not the only or the most important false claim made about wind energy. Other false claims about wind energy include the following:

- It is low or competitive in cost. In fact, its cost is high when all true costs are counted.
- It is environmentally benign. In fact, it has significant adverse environmental, ecological, scenic, and property value impacts.
- It avoids significant emissions that would otherwise be produced. In fact, it avoids few.
- It provides big job and economic benefits. In fact, there are few such benefits.
- It reduces U.S. dependence on imported oil. In fact, it does not.
- It reduces the need for building reliable generating units in areas experiencing growth in peak electricity demand or needing to replace old generating units. The opposite is true.

Such claims as these have been made often during the past decade and more by the wind industry and other wind advocates. Only during the past 3–4 years have these claims begun to be demonstrated as false and misleading. The facts about wind energy are beginning to show up in the media but, unfortunately, have yet to be understood by most political leaders and regulators.

FOURTEEN

Wave Power Could Become a Good Alternative for Making Electricity

Stan Freeman

Stan Freeman is a journalist for the *Republican* newspaper in Springfield, Massachusetts. In the following viewpoint Freeman provides a brief overview of water as a power source. He compares different approaches to creating electricity by harnessing the power of naturally occurring waves and tides and compares water power to wind power. Freeman presents the idea that water power is the most reliable source of alternative energy.

In the fall of 1884, when water flowing over the Holyoke Dam was first harnessed to create electricity, the feat was considered a wonder of human invention. "Boys were playing marbles on the streets of Holyoke at nine o'clock in the evening under the illumination of the electric lights," a newspaper of the time noted.

Before geothermal and biodiesel, before photovoltaic cells and hydrogen fuel cells, there was water power. Long before. More than 2,000 years ago, the Greeks were using water wheels to grind wheat into flour.

But what's old may be what's new.

Water Power Is Reliable

Because of global warming, the need for non-polluting sources of energy to replace fossil fuels is growing in its urgency. So the push is on to find new or more efficient ways to take advantage of the most reliable source of energy on the planet, water power. After all, the sun doesn't always shine and the wind doesn't always blow, but tides rise and fall and rivers flow virtually without pause.

"Of all the renewables, the most predictable are the tides in the ocean. If the tides give out, it means you have much bigger problems. You've lost the moon or the sun," said John Topping, of the Washington, D.C.–based Massachusetts Tidal Energy. His organization has been granted a federal permit to investigate putting up to 100 underwater turbines in the waters off Martha's Vineyard that would run on the movement of the tides.

By contrast, water power on rivers has just about been exploited to its limits. In all of New England, there are perhaps 500 megawatts of power left to be coaxed from good hydroelectric sites, primarily abandoned or unused dams, on rivers and streams (the equivalent power of one large coal-fired power plant).

And that's assuming environmentalists will not fight the effort, according to Peter B. Clark, president of Swift River Hydro in Hamilton. In fact, the campaign now among environmentalists is to remove unused dams, he said.

"The big push for small hydro occurred back in the late '70s and early '80s when a lot of people did the bigger projects on the Connecticut River and elsewhere. The larger and more effective sites were licensed at that time," Clark said.

Clark's company developed some of the small hydropower sites in New England, locations that produced a few megawatts each, and he hopes to develop some of the remaining potentially productive sites. "A lot of industries used water power for the last century around New England, and what remains of that are the dams that have been abandoned and the old power houses. There may be 30 or 40 towns that have old dams that no one knows what to do with," he said.

Hydroelectric-generating plants, like this one in New England, use water power to generate electricity. Water, says the author, is the most reliable power source on earth.

One of the company's projects is at the former Strathmore Paper Co. Woronoco dam on the Westfield River in Russell [Massachusetts]. In 2001, Swift River Hydro signed a contract to maintain and operate the hydroelectric project at the dam. Hydropower—in the form of water wheels—was first developed in that part of the river in the early 1870s.

Using state financing set aside for renewable energy projects, Swift River Hydro is working to add additional turbines at the dam. The dam is already capable of producing about 1.7 megawatts of electricity that is sold to the Western Massachusetts Electric Co. But once the work is finished, the hydroelectric station's output would be 3.7 megawatts, producing enough electricity to power perhaps 2,000 to 3,000 homes.

However, the dam actually has the potential for 5 megawatts, said William K. Fay, an owner of Swift River Hydro along with Clark. "There is room for expansion at some of these sites that have been developed. In some cases, a substantial amount of capacity could be added. There are also some sites out there that were uneconomical to develop [at] the lower power prices" that might be economical to develop now that prices have risen, he said.

Water Power Can Be Developed Further

In 1995, the U.S. Department of Energy identified 130 sites on rivers and streams in Massachusetts that had a realistic potential to produce hydropower, for a total output of 132 megawatts. (As a reference, the hydroelectric station at the Holyoke Dam produces 43.8 megawatts.) Nearly 70 of the sites identified were in the Connecticut River water basin, with the collective potential to produce about 80 megawatts. Many were at small neglected dams on tributaries, and most of the sites were only capable of producing 1 megawatt of power or less.

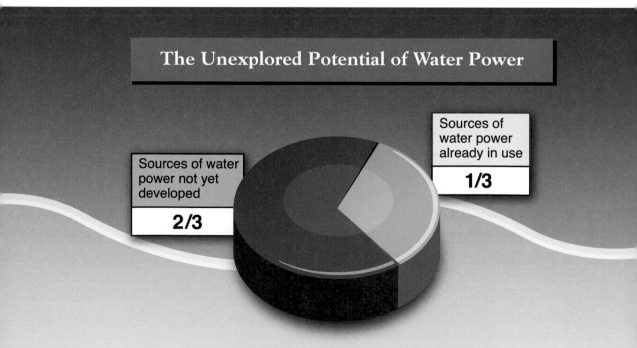

The Unexplored Potential of Water Power

Sources of water power not yet developed

2/3

Sources of water power already in use

1/3

Taken from: U.S. Geological Survey, 2009. http://ga.water.usgs.gov/edu/wuhy.html.

Historically, good use has been made of the rivers in Western Massachusetts in the production of power. In all of Massachusetts, there exists nearly 1,800 megawatts of hydroelectric capacity, and nearly all of it is produced in the four western counties. (One megawatt is enough power for about 1,000 homes.)

Just two projects, the Bear Swamp pumped storage facility in the Franklin County town of Rowe and its neighboring town Florida on the Deerfield River and the Northfield Mountain pumped storage facility on the Connecticut River, account for about 1,600 megawatts of that electricity. At both facilities, water is pumped into an elevated reservoir when the power demand and the cost to pump it are low, and then it is released into turbines when demand and the price paid for the electricity are high.

In addition to the hydroelectric station at the Holyoke Dam, there is a station at Turners Falls in Montague that generates about 67 megawatts, and several small stations on the Deerfield and Westfield rivers, generally under 10 megawatts each.

In the final analysis, the new frontier for hydropower appears to be on Massachusetts' coast, said James F. Manwell, director of the Renewable Energy Research Laboratory at University of Massachusetts in Amherst. "With tidal and ocean power (harnessing the motion of waves), there is hope. But the applications are definitely limited. For tidal power, you have to find a spot where the tide is significant," he said.

Comparing Tidal Power and Wave Power

Water power relies on moving water. Falling water tends to have more potential to produce electricity than flowing water, though. The speed that a mass of water falling from 25 feet or more can achieve tends to be greater than the speed of a river current. So typically, a river is dammed, creating a body of water behind the dam that is at a higher elevation than the water in front of it. Water is then allowed to fall from the higher reservoir to the lower one through a turbine, turning its wheels and generating electricity. The same can be done at a waterfall of any size, such as Niagara Falls.

Waves are also a consistent source of small amounts of power. At best, such a system would likely be able to power little more than a buoy lamp. For instance, the up and down motion of a buoy tethered to the ocean floor could move a piston that turns a generator, creating electricity. Since these wave systems would be on or near the ocean surface, though, they would be a hazard to ships, so to array thousands of them in order to extract a significant amount of power would likely not appeal to the shipping and boating communities.

There are two primary ways the ocean tides are employed to create electricity. One method is to capture the water of a high tide in a reservoir, close the gate, and when the tide goes out, to release the water into a turbine. The other method is to put an array of small turbines underwater that turn as the rising or falling tide moves water in a particular direction.

Massachusetts Tidal Energy is investigating the second method for its project in Vineyard Sound, putting turbines underwater that are smaller versions of the wind turbines seen on land. The blades will cut a circle about 35 feet in diameter and will sit on the ocean floor in about 75 feet of water. Each turbine—from 50 to 100 of them—will generate one half to two megawatts of power.

"In the case of tides, you don't have 24-hour-a-day electricity, but you may have 20 hours. However, for the next 1,000 years you know the hours and minutes each day when you will have power. That's good for a utility. What they need is predictability," Topping said.

Comparing Water Power and Wind Energy

While wind turbines turn swiftly enough that they can endanger birds, the blades on underwater turbines move so slowly that they pose no threat to fish, he said. "Also, they don't create the problems that folks at Cape Wind (the proposed wind farm in the waters off Nantucket) have. People don't want to see anything. The advantage of tidal power is that it's out of sight, out of mind. And if you use the right technology, it is about as benign as possible environmentally," Topping said.

A major problem with the various forms of ocean hydroelectric is that they are new and untested, said Manwell. "A lot of ocean energy technologies are hampered because it's expensive to get started. With the early wind turbines, they had lots of problems. But they slowly worked them out. They have all that experience on land. But with water turbines, you just have to jump in. You don't have experience to build on. So it's tough. The first time you do anything, it's always more expensive than you think," he said.

Despite the high initial starting cost, ocean turbines, along with all renewable energy technologies, have an advantage over fossil-fuel generated power, said Clark, of Swift River Hydro. "The Achilles' heel of a natural gas (fueled power plant) is fuel prices. We don't have that. We have a big first cost, as do most renewables. But the point is we don't have the recurring costs of fuel. The world conditions change. There were a lot of gas turbine plants that had to shut down a few years ago when gas prices were high," he said.

FIFTEEN

Geothermal Power Could Become a Good Alternative for Making Electricity

Ken Silverstein

Ken Silverstein is the editor in chief for *EnergyBiz Insider*. In the following viewpoint Silverstein provides an overview of geothermal power. He discusses the process used to harness naturally occurring heat from the earth's core and looks at pros and cons for using geothermal energy in different places. Silverstein presents the idea that geothermal power has the potential to become a reliable alternative energy source.

It now makes up just a sliver of the electricity generation pie. But experts at the Massachusetts Institute of Technology [MIT] say that enhanced geothermal systems (EGS) could have far wider applications and be especially useful in times of high energy prices and carbon constraints. Not only are the systems much cleaner than fossil fuels but they also provide a continuous flow of energy—all at competitive prices.

"Geothermal energy could play an important role in our national energy picture as a non-carbon-based energy source," says

Ken Silverstein, "Geothermal Energy's Potential," *EnergyBiz Insider*, August 22, 2008. www.energycentral.com/centers/energybiz/ebi_list.cfm. Copyright © 1996–2009 by CyberTech, Inc. Reproduced by permission.

Nafi Toksoz, professor of geophysics at MIT. "It's a very large resource and has the potential to be a significant contributor to the energy needs of this country." Geothermal now provides less than 1 percent of the world's power, he says, although it could supply as much as 20 percent in the coming decades.

How Geothermal Power Works

To get there, the MIT panel says that the tools to perfect deep drilling and water flow through the underground navigation system are needed. MIT Engineering Professor Jeff Tester and panel member David Blackwell, professor of geophysics at Southern Methodist University in Texas, also point out that geothermal resources are available nationwide. But the highest-grade sites are in western states where hot rocks are closer to the surface, requiring less drilling and thereby reducing exploration costs.

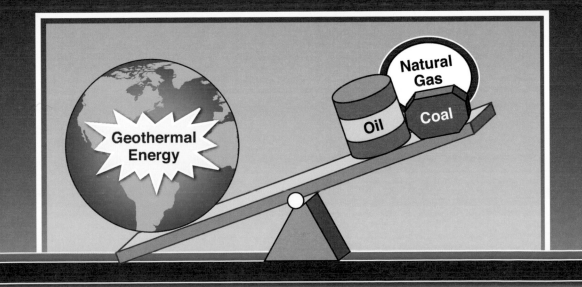

The Potential of Geothermal Energy

Government surveys have estimated that the amount of untapped potential geothermal energy is larger than the amount of coal, oil, and natural gas combined.

The EGS study says that several wells must be drilled to reach those hot rocks. Once there, those wells must then be linked with natural or induced fractures in the rock to allow the water to flow through. Water is pumped via the wells through these fractures in the hot rock and up to the surface to run electric generators at the surface. Unlike conventional fossil-fuel power plants that burn coal, natural gas or oil, no fuel would be required. To that end, the panel says that the environmental effects of geothermal power are "markedly lower" than either fossil fuels or nuclear power. And unlike wind and solar systems, a geothermal plant works night and day.

"This environmental advantage is due to low emissions and the small overall footprint of the entire geothermal system, which results because energy capture and extraction is contained entirely underground, and the surface equipment needed for conversion to electricity is relatively compact," says Tester.

Pros and Cons for Commercial Use

It's not an easy objective. It costs a lot of money to drill wells in large part because explorers need to drill deep into the earth, often 5,000 feet or more below the earth's surface.

MIT's report also notes that meeting water requirements for geothermal plants may be an issue, particularly in arid regions. Further, the water that is used to create electricity must be kept separate from drinking water supplies to prevent contamination. Additionally, the potential for seismic risk from fluid injection needs to be carefully monitored. The cumulative effect of all those obstacles has led skeptics to conclude that geothermal energy will remain a nominal power source.

Others, however, are more upbeat. Some of the same technologies now being used by the oil and gas industries to minimize their environmental footprints can be applied to drilling wells to create geothermal energy. In a carbon constrained world, companies would have the incentive to make such investments.

"The possibility of drilling into these rocks, fracturing them and pumping water in to produce steam has already been shown

Workers move a generator into place at the Raser Technologies geothermal plant, enabling the plant to produce geothermal power for 9,000 homes in nearby Minersville, Utah.

to be feasible," says MIT's Toksoz. He emphasizes that the same concept could be replicated throughout the nation but that advanced tools are necessary so that it could all be accomplished in commercial-scale.

Uses for Homes, Businesses, and Schools

Ground source heat pumps are another form of geothermal energy that can be tapped into by households and businesses to meet their heating and cooling needs. In this application, pipes are buried in the ground at a depth where the temperature of the earth remains constant, usually several meters.

Because the earth's temperature is always moderate at 50–60 degrees Fahrenheit, these types of heating and cooling systems are less stressed than conventional ones. That conserves a lot of energy when compared to units that use centralized air and heat. Monthly savings could total somewhere between 25 percent and 50 percent of current utility bills. And that's why the federal government has a goal of getting 7 million homes and businesses to use geothermal heat pumps by 2010.

In New Mexico, schools are being retrofitted with geothermal heat pumps that developers say will save as much as 50 percent on energy bills. And the Little Rock, Ark. region is installing geothermal units at several fire stations and one police outpost. Several schools in Iowa have geothermal heating and cooling systems, as well as at least one in Wisconsin.

Of course, these are pricey too. The U.S. Department of Energy pegs an average home installation at about US $7,500. While that is more than a conventional heating and cooling system, the DOE claims that depending on factors such as climate, soil conditions, system features and financing and incentives, homeowners can expect to recoup their investment in anywhere between two and ten years.

Now that energy topics are taking center stage in the [2008] presidential debate, it would be remiss of the candidates not to discuss the possibilities of geothermal energy. Like any burgeoning energy form, it must endure several impediments while also attracting a sizable investment to allow it to reach a critical mass. With several projects underway, the process has begun.

What You Should Know About Alternative Energy

What Is Alternative Energy?

Energy is power that can be used to generate electricity, operate machinery, move cars and trucks, heat or cool a building, and so on. The sources of energy most often used in the United States today are oil, coal, and natural gas. These are known as fossil fuels because they are taken from the fossilized remains of ancient plants and animals that lived millions of years ago. Because a limited amount of fossil fuel exists within the earth, and more cannot be created easily, fossil fuels are considered nonrenewable energy sources.

Alternative energy is any source of energy that replaces or supplements fossil fuels. Alternative energy sources are renewable, meaning that the supply of potential energy is unlimited or can be easily replenished within a relatively short time. Natural forces such as sunlight and wind are considered renewable energy sources because the supply cannot be used up. Trees and plants are also considered renewable sources of energy because when they are used, more can be grown. Some examples of alternative energy sources are:

- solar power: Sunlight used for heat or to make electricity.
- wind power: Moving air currents used to drive machinery or to make electricity.
- geothermal energy: The internal heat of the earth's core, used for heating or to make electricity.

- water power, or hydropower: Moving water used to drive machinery or to make electricity.
- wave power: A form of water power that uses the energy of ocean waves to drive machinery or to make electricity.
- tidal power: A form of water power that uses the energy of tides in lakes or the ocean to drive machinery or to make electricity.
- biofuel: Organic matter (collectively known as biomass) that can be burned as fuel or made into fuel. Some examples of biofuels are:
  - wood
  - ethanol made from corn or sugar cane
  - biodiesel made from fat or vegetable oil
  - methanol made from wood
  - algae and other water plants
  - peat (partially decayed plant matter)
  - garbage and trash
  - manure

Facts About Alternative Energy

- Two hundred years ago 90 percent of the energy needed in the United States came from wood and the muscle power of humans and farm animals such as horses, mules, and oxen.
- Today fossil fuels supply more than 90 percent of the energy used in the United States:
  - oil and petroleum supply 40 percent;
  - natural gas, 23 percent;
  - coal, 22 percent;
  - nuclear power, 8 percent.
- Alternative energy sources supply only 7 percent of the energy used in the United States today. Of that 7 percent:
  - biofuels supply 53 percent;
  - water power, 36 percent;
  - wind energy, 5 percent;
  - geothermal energy, 5 percent;
  - solar energy, 1 percent.

- More than half of the energy used in the United States today is for making electricity. Most of this electricity is made with fossil fuels:
    - burning coal supplies 48.5 percent;
    - burning natural gas, 21.6 percent;
    - burning petroleum (oil), 2 percent;
    - nuclear power, 19.4 percent;
    - water power, 5.8 percent;
    - burning biofuels, 1 percent;
    - geothermal power, less than 1 percent;
    - solar power, less than 1 percent;
    - wind power, less than 1 percent.
- Homes use 37 percent of electricity;
- businesses, 36 percent;
- industrial purposes, 27 percent;
- transportation vehicles, less than 1 percent.

According to a survey conducted in 2008 by ABC News and Planet Green, 64 percent of Americans believe that it is important to find new energy sources as alternatives to fossil fuels. Many Americans believe that the environment is being harmed by the excessive carbon emissions that result from using oil and other fossil fuels. The United States is one of the world's largest consumers of fossil fuels and is therefore responsible for a large amount of carbon emissions. The Web site MoveBeyondOil provides statistics on the use of oil in the United States:

- The United States uses 25 percent of the world's oil, the most of any country in the world and an amount equal to the five next largest oil-consuming countries combined.
- Every day, the United States uses twenty-one million barrels of oil, each containing forty-two gallons.
- The United States uses 7.5 billion barrels of oil each year.
- Nearly 70 percent of U.S. oil consumption is used for transportation vehicles.
- Nearly three-fourths of the U.S. oil used for transportation is for gasoline in cars and SUVs.
- The amount of fuel consumed in these vehicles each year would fill a swimming pool as big as a football field and forty miles deep.

What You Should Do About Alternative Energy

Know Your Energy Needs

To understand alternative energy and decide if it can work for you, first you must know something about the energy you are already using. People use energy everywhere: at home, school, and work, in businesses, factories, and stores, and to travel to all of these places. The type of energy that is used depends on what people are doing, where they are doing it, and other factors such as the weather, the season of the year, the time of day or night, and whether they are in a city or in a rural area. Knowing how, where, and when you use energy is the first step in evaluating the best source of energy for your needs.

When thinking about how you use energy, ask yourself these questions:

- How far do you travel to get to places you go frequently, such as to school, stores, or a friend's house? Are these places nearby or very far from your home? The amount of energy used for traveling depends partly on the length of the trip.
- How do you usually travel to places away from home? Do you walk, ride a bike, take a bus, ride in a car, or do you travel in some other way? Different amounts and types of energy are used depending on the method of travel.
- Do you live in a place where it gets very cold or very warm? Home heating and cooling are two of the biggest uses of energy in the United States.
- Do you spend more time doing things indoors or outside? Different types and amounts of energy may be used depending on where you are.
- Do you do most things during the day or after dark? Nighttime activities may use more energy for lighting.

- Do your favorite things to do require electricity? Remember electricity is needed to power lights, television, video games, computers, wireless phones, and all sorts of other machines. Most batteries count as electricity too.

Online energy calculators, like those at the Web sites listed below, can also help you understand how much energy you use.

- www.h2oconserve.org
- www.nwf.org/water/watercalculator.cfm
- www.consumerspower.org/home_energy/billestimator.php
- www.mygreenelectronics.org/EnergyCalculator.aspx

Explore Your Energy Alternatives

There are many forms of alternative energy, and each type works in a specific way. Some alternative energy sources work best for making electricity or charging batteries, while others work best for capturing heat or powering machinery and vehicles.

Once you have an idea of what your energy needs are, you can explore alternative energy sources to decide if any of them could work for you or your household.

When thinking about how you or your household might be able to use alternative sources of energy, answer questions like these:

- Do you live in a place that is sunny most of the time? Some solar panels can produce electricity even on cloudy days. The smallest solar panels can even be used indoors to collect sunlight from a window and use it to charge batteries.
- Do you live in a place where the wind blows most days? Some smaller wind turbines need an average wind speed of only nine miles per hour to function.
- Is your home surrounded by tall trees or other buildings? Or is your home open to natural elements like sunshine or wind? Solar panels and wind turbines need open space in order to gather sunlight and catch passing air currents.

Noticing how alternative energy is used in your neighborhood or community can also help you decide if it would be a good choice for you or your household. If you know anyone who uses alternative energy at home or work, like a family member, neighbors, or friend, ask them about it. Talking to someone who has experience using alternative energy is one of the best ways to learn about the benefits and drawbacks of a specific energy source. If you do not know anyone who uses alternative energy, ask a teacher or another adult if someone with alternative energy experience can visit your school, classroom, or other group meeting to talk about it.

Starting conversations about alternative energy at school or in your community can be the beginning of a grassroots effort to educate others and encourage schools or organizations to explore such energy sources. You can take such efforts further by organizing an e-mail campaign to your elected representatives, urging them to enact legislation that reflects your views on alternative energies.

ORGANIZATIONS TO CONTACT

The editors have compiled the following list of organizations concerned with the issues debated in this book. The descriptions are derived from materials provided by the organizations. All have publications or information available for interested readers. The list was compiled on the date of publication of the present volume; the information provided here may change. Be aware that many organizations take several weeks or longer to respond to inquiries, so allow as much time as possible for the receipt of requested materials.

American Coalition for Ethanol (ACE)
5000 S. Broadband Ln., Ste. 224, Sioux Falls, SD 57108
(605) 334-3381
Web site: www.ethanol.org

ACE is a national organization of individuals and businesses involved in the production of fuel ethanol. The group's primary goals are to reduce America's dependence on imported oil, to educate consumers about the benefits of fuel ethanol, to correct misconceptions about ethanol, and to support increased production and use of ethanol. Its Web site provides information related to fuel ethanol, including facts, statistics, news, laws, reports, brochures, and publications.

American Nuclear Society
555 N. Kensington Ave., La Grange Park, IL 60526
(708) 352-6611; (800) 323-3044
e-mail: outreach@ans.org
Web site: www.aboutnuclear.org

The American Nuclear Society is a scientific educational organization that promotes the awareness and understanding of nuclear science and technology. Its Web site provides extensive information for students, focusing on the use of nuclear technology applications in five major fields: food irradiation, industry, medicine, space, and electricity.

American Solar Energy Society (ASES)
2400 Central Ave., Ste. A, Boulder, CO 80301
(303) 443-3130
e-mail: ases@ases.org
Web site: www.ases.org

The ASES is a nonprofit membership organization for solar energy professionals and advocates. The society promotes the increased use of solar energy in the United States and sponsors programs such as the National Solar Tour, a large grassroots educational event focusing on solar energy, energy efficiency, and climate change. Its Web site includes information about solar energy, energy efficiency, and other sustainable technologies, and a collection of news stories related to solar energy.

American Wind Energy Association (AWEA)
1501 M St. NW, Ste. 1000, Washington, DC 20005
(202) 383-2500
e-mail: windmail@awea.org
Web site: www.awea.org

The AWEA is a national membership organization for wind energy professionals and advocates. Its primary goal is to promote wind energy as a clean source of electricity for consumers. Its Web site provides extensive information about wind energy in the United States and other countries, including facts and statistics about wind energy, climate change, and related topics. An online resource library includes downloadable fact sheets, reports, and multimedia materials.

Breakthrough Generation
c/o The Breakthrough Institute,
Rockefeller Philanthropy Advisors
437 Madison Ave., 37th Fl., New York, NY 10022
Web site: breakthroughgen.org

Breakthrough Generation focuses on the development of youth leadership for the advancement of creative, large-scale solutions to America's critical energy issues. Its Web site includes a blog and publications library with links to reports, case studies, student action toolkits, and news stories related to climate change.

Clean and Safe Energy Coalition (CASE)
(202) 338-2273
e-mail: director@casenergy.org
Web site: www.cleansafeenergy.org

CASE is a grassroots political action organization that promotes nuclear energy as a safe and dependable source of electricity. Its Web site provides information on energy security, clean air quality, and current news and issues related to nuclear energy. Resources and statistics on the use of nuclear energy in each state are also provided.

Electric Auto Association
e-mail: contact@eaaev.org
Web site: electricauto.org

The Electric Auto Association is a nonprofit educational organization that promotes electric and hybrid vehicles as clean, quiet, and practical alternatives to cars and trucks powered by gas and diesel fuels. Its Web site provides facts, statistics, reports, and publications about electric vehicles, including the history of plug-in cars. An online discussion forum, newsletter archive, and information about local chapters and upcoming events are also available on the Web site.

Energy Action Coalition
1718 Twenty-first St. NW, Washington, DC 20036
(202) 328-1733
e-mail: theteam@energyaction.net
Web site: www.energyactioncoalition.org

The Energy Action Coalition is a network of fifty youth and student groups working for clean energy in North America. Its

Web site includes information about current and past campaigns and actions, energy action blogs, and links to related news stories.

Industrial Wind Action Group
e-mail: info@windaction.org
Web site: www.windaction.org

The Industrial Wind Action Group is opposed to wind energy. The group works to educate lawmakers and the public about the negative effects of wind energy installations on the environment, economy, and quality of life in residential areas. Its Web site provides a multimedia resource library of information about the limitations of wind power as an alternative energy source and its ineffectiveness at reducing carbon emissions.

National Biodiesel Board
605 Clark Ave., Jefferson City, MO 65101
(573) 635-3893
e-mail: info@biodiesel.org
Web site: www.biodiesel.org

The National Biodiesel Board represents the U.S. biodiesel industry by coordinating research and development of biodiesel fuel. Its mission is to promote biodiesel fuel as a clean, renewable, domestically produced alternative energy source. Its Web site provides print and multimedia information on myths and facts about biodiesel fuel and its uses, food versus fuel sustainability, fuel fact sheets, and related publications.

Natural Resources Defense Council
40 W. Twentieth St., New York, NY 10011
(212) 727-2700
e-mail: nrdcinfo@nrdc.org
Web site: www.nrdc.org

The Natural Resources Defense Council is a grassroots environmental action group that works to protect wildlife, ensure a healthy environment, reduce global warming, and promote clean energy. Its Web site provides information about environmental concerns, U.S. environmental laws and policies, environmental justice, green living, and green business practices. An online activist network provides information about current action campaigns and tools for individual action.

1Sky
6930 Carroll Ave., Ste. 1000, Takoma Park, MD 20912
(301) 270-4550
e-mail: info@1sky.org
Web site: www.1sky.org

1Sky is a grassroots political activism organization that promotes oil independence, renewable energy, and a shift to a green economy. 1Sky lobbies the U.S. government to take action to stop global warming. Its Web site provides information on joining or starting a local chapter and how to participate in upcoming events. The Web site also includes a blog, online discussion forum, and a resource library covering a wide range of topics related to clean energy and climate change. Downloadable posters and action guides are also available.

Plug-In America
309A Steiner St., San Francisco, CA 94117
(415) 252-7162
e-mail: info@pluginamerica.org
Web site: www.pluginamerica.org

Plug-In America is a network of individuals dedicated to promoting the use of plug-in electric vehicles as a way to reduce America's dependence on imported oil. Members work to raise awareness of the benefits of battery electric and plug-in hybrid vehicles. Its Web site includes an action center with information on things that individuals can do to support the use of electric cars. Other Web site resources include extensive information about electric and plug-in hybrid vehicle technology, e-mail newsletters and action alerts, podcasts, multimedia library, and a news archive.

Plug-In Partners

c/o Partnership Services Coordinator
721 Barton Springs Rd., Austin, TX 78704
(512) 322-6511
e-mail: contact@pluginpartners.com
Web site: www.pluginpartners.com

Plug-In Partners is a national grassroots organization that campaigns to convince auto companies that car buyers are interested in purchasing flexible-fuel plug-in hybrid electric vehicles. Its Web site includes facts and statistics about plug-in hybrid electric vehicles, a library of related news stories, and a downloadable action kit that individuals can use to start a local awareness campaign.

Renewable Fuels Association (RFA)

1 Massachusetts Ave. NW, Ste. 820, Washington, DC 20001
(202) 289-3835
Web site: www.ethanolrfa.org

The RFA is a national trade organization for professionals in the U.S. ethanol industry. The association promotes research and development projects that support the increased production and use of fuel ethanol. Its Web site provides information about ethanol, including a special section for students and teachers.

Repower America

c/o Alliance for Climate Protection
901 E St. NW, Washington, DC 20004
Web site: www.repoweramerica.org

Repower America is a project of the Alliance for Climate Protection. This grassroots awareness campaign works to educate the public about clean energy, the need for reduced greenhouse gas emissions, and alternatives to imported oil. Its Web site provides information on energy efficiency, renewable sources of electricity, local electricity generation, alternative fuels for cars, and simple actions that individuals can participate in within local communities.

Set America Free
7811 Montrose Rd., Ste. 505, Potomac, MD 20854
(866) 713-7527
e-mail: info@setamericafree.org
Web site: www.setamericafree.org

Set America Free is a coalition of organizations and individuals concerned about America's dependence on imported oil. The coalition works to educate people about the dangers of dependence on imported oil, the need for alternative fuels, the benefits of flexible-fuel vehicles, and the importance of public policies that support alternative fuels. Its Web site includes an explanation of myths and facts about U.S. oil consumption and oil independence, links to related news stories and blog postings, and an action center.

Solar Nation
c/o Green America
1612 K St. NW, Ste. 600, Washington, DC 20006
Web site: www.solar-nation.org

Solar Nation is a nonprofit energy activism organization that works to change U.S. energy policies to focus more on solar power. Its Web site includes information and statistics related to energy usage, energy efficiency, and renewable energy, with a particular emphasis on the advantages and technology of solar power. Information about current and past action campaigns is also provided.

350.org
The David Brewer Center, Ste. 340, Berkeley, CA 94704
(510) 250-7860
Web site: www.350.org

350.org is a global action network uniting more than two hundred member organizations around the world. Through grassroots organizing and activism, the network promotes the creation and adoption of international solutions to reduce the carbon emissions that cause global warming. The network takes its name from 350ppm (parts per million), the number representing the maximum amount of carbon dioxide that can safely exist in Earth's atmosphere. Its Web site includes action ideas and organizing plans, downloadable posters, fliers, stencils, and a special section for youth activism.

Union of Concerned Scientists
2 Brattle Sq., Cambridge, MA 02238
(617) 547-5552
Web site: www.ucsusa.org

The Union of Concerned Scientists is a nonprofit alliance of scientists, teachers, students, and members of the general public. The group uses independent scientific research and activism to encourage changes in government policy, corporate practices, and consumer choices that support clean energy and a healthier environment. Its Web site includes information on current and pending legislation related to environmental issues and an extensive resource library of fact sheets, letters, position papers, publications, news stories, and more.

Windustry
2105 First Ave. S., Minneapolis, MN 55404
(612) 870-3461; (800) 946-3640
e-mail: info@windustry.org
Web site: www.windustry.org

Windustry is a national nonprofit organization that promotes wind power as a renewable alternative energy. The organization works to develop community-based wind energy projects, operates an information hotline, produces educational materials, and sponsors events to raise public awareness of the benefits of wind energy. Its Web site provides facts and research reports about wind power, a glossary of related terms, and a searchable online resource library.

BIBLIOGRAPHY

Books

Tom Blees, *Prescription for the Planet: The Painless Remedy for Our Energy and Environmental Crises*. Charleston, SC: BookSurge, 2008.

Sherry Boschert, *Plug-in Hybrids: The Cars That Will Recharge America*. Gabriola Island, BC: New Society, 2006.

Michael Brune, *Coming Clean: Breaking America's Addiction to Oil and Coal*. San Francisco: Sierra Club, 2008.

Robert Bryce, *Gusher of Lies: The Dangerous Delusions of Energy Independence*. New York: Public Affairs, 2008.

Helen Caldicott, *Nuclear Power Is Not the Answer*. New York: New Press, 2006.

David Craddock, *Renewable Energy Made Easy: Free Energy from Solar, Wind, Hydropower, and Other Alternative Energy Sources*. Ocala, FL: Atlantic, 2008.

Gwyneth Cravens and Richard Rhodes, *Power to Save the World: The Truth About Nuclear Energy*. New York: Knopf, 2007.

Rik DeGunther, *Alternative Energy for Dummies*. Hoboken, NJ: Wiley, 2009.

Morgan Downey, *Oil 101*. New York: Wooden Table, 2009.

Thomas L. Friedman, *Hot, Flat, and Crowded: Why We Need a Green Revolution—and How It Can Renew America*. New York: Farrar, Straus, and Giroux, 2008.

Stan Gibilisco, *Alternative Energy Demystified*. New York: McGraw-Hill Professional, 2006.

Jeff Goodell, *Big Coal: The Dirty Secret Behind America's Energy Future*. Wilmington, MA: Mariner, 2007.

Howard C. Hayden, *The Solar Fraud: Why Solar Energy Won't Run the World*. Pueblo West, CO: Vales Lake, 2005.

Alan M. Herbst and George W. Hopley, *Nuclear Energy Now: Why the Time Has Come for the World's Most Misunderstood Energy Source*. Hoboken, NJ: Wiley, 2007.

Miriam Horn and Fred Krupp, *Earth: The Sequel: The Race to Reinvent Energy and Stop Global Warming*. New York: Norton, 2008.

Christopher C. Horner, *Red Hot Lies: How Global Warming Alarmists Use Threats, Fraud, and Deception to Keep You Misinformed*. Washington, DC: Regnery, 2008.

Michael T. Klare, *Blood and Oil: The Dangers and Consequences of America's Growing Dependency on Imported Petroleum*. New York: Holt Paperbacks, 2005.

David J.C. MacKay, *Sustainable Energy—Without the Hot Air*. Cambridge: UIT Cambridge, 2009.

Arjun Makhijani, *Carbon-Free and Nuclear-Free: A Roadmap for U.S. Energy Policy*. Muskegon, MI: RDR, 2007.

Robin M. Mills, *The Myth of the Oil Crisis: Overcoming the Challenges of Depletion, Geopolitics, and Global Warming*. Santa Barbara, CA: Praeger, 2008.

Jack R. Nerad, *The Complete Idiot's Guide to Hybrid and Alternative Fuel Vehicles*. New York: Alpha, 2007.

Joe Shuster, *Beyond Fossil Fools: The Roadmap to Energy Independence by 2040*. Minneapolis: Beaver's Pond, 2008.

Vaclav Smil, *Energy: A Beginner's Guide*. Oxford: Oneworld, 2006.
———, *Oil: A Beginner's Guide*. Oxford: Oneworld, 2008.

Brice Smith, *Insurmountable Risks: The Dangers of Using Nuclear Power to Combat Global Climate Change*. Muskegon, MI: RDR, 2006.

Lawrence Solomon, *The Deniers: The World Renowned Scientists Who Stood Up Against Global Warming Hysteria, Political Persecution, and Fraud*. Minneapolis: Richard Vigilante, 2008.

William Tucker, *Terrestrial Energy: How Nuclear Energy Will Lead the Green Revolution and End America's Energy Odyssey*. Savage, MD: Bartleby, 2008.

Wendy Williams and Robert Whitcomb, *Cape Wind: Money, Celebrity, Class, Politics and the Battle for Our Energy Future*. Cambridge, MA: Public Affairs, 2007.

Richard Wolfson, *Energy, Environment, and Climate*. New York: Norton, 2008.

Periodicals

Jerry Adler, "Going Green: With Windmills, Low-Energy Homes, New Forms of Recycling and Fuel-Efficient Cars, Americans Are Taking Conservation into Their Own Hands," *Newsweek*, July 17, 2006.

Jeffrey Ball, "A Big Sum of Small Differences: Individual Americans Cause—and Could Cure—Most of U.S. Emissions Problem," *Wall Street Journal*, October 2, 2008.

Joshua Boak, "Ethanol vs. Food Debate Growing," *Chicago Tribune*, May 1, 2008.

Kenneth Chang, "Scientists Would Turn Greenhouse Gas into Gasoline," *New York Times*, February 19, 2008.

Gregory Dicum, "Plugging into the Sun," *New York Times*, January 4, 2007.

Sandi Doughton, "Tapping Tidal Energy: The Wave of the Future," *Seattle Times*, October 7, 2007.

John Farrell, "On Renewable Energy, Go Local," *Minneapolis-St. Paul (MN) Star-Tribune*, August 15, 2007.

Kent Garber, "In the Push for Alternative Energy, What Happened to Geothermal?" *U.S. News & World Report*, July 21, 2008.

Scott Gibson, "Solar Energy: Why It's Better than Ever," *Mother Earth News*, August/September 2008.

Michael Grunwald, "The Clean Energy Scam," *Time*, April 7, 2008.

Jerry Harkavy, "Turbines Harness to Predictable Tides," *Charleston (WV) Gazette*, September 7, 2008.

Fran Korten, "Time to Get Smart About Energy," *Yes!* May 30, 2006.

Jim Motavalli, "A Nuclear Phoenix? Concern About Climate Change Is Spurring an Atomic Renaissance," *E/The Environmental Magazine*, July/August 2007.

Jad Mouawad, "Pumping Hydrogen," *New York Times*, September 23, 2008.

Natural Life, "Are Wind Turbines Dangerous?" July/August 2007.

Michelle Nijhuis, "Selling the Wind: Wind Power Is Pollution-Free, Combats Global Warming, and Is a Boon to Small Farmers," *Audubon*, September/October 2006.

Ron Pernick, "Clean Energy: It's Getting Affordable," *Business Week*, March 18, 2008.

Romano Prodi, "Biofuels Can't Feed Starving People," *Christian Science Monitor*, April 29, 2008.

Ryan Randazzo, "Off the Grid, in the Desert, Residents Generate All Forms of Alternative Energy to Maintain Their Lifestyle," *Arizona Republic*, February 10, 2008.

Matthew L. Wald, "Efficiency, Not Just Alternatives, Is Promoted as an Energy Saver," *New York Times*, May 29, 2007.

———, "Challenging Gasoline: Diesel, Ethanol, Hydrogen," *New York Times*, October 24, 2007.

Jeff Wise, "The Truth About Hydrogen," *Popular Mechanics*, November 2006.

Mortimer B. Zuckerman, "Stop the Energy Insanity," *U.S. News & World Report*, July 21, 2008.

Internet Sources

Lester Brown, "Starving for Fuel: How Ethanol Production Contributes to Global Hunger," *Globalist*, August 2, 2006. www.theglobalist.com/storyid.aspx?StoryId=5518.

Robert Bryce, "Ethanol Is the Agricultural Equivalent of Holy Water," *Washington Spectator*, June 15, 2007. www.washingtonspectator.org/Articles/SF_501626323.cfm.

Antrim Caskey, "Big Coal's Dirty Plans for Our Energy Future," AlterNet, December 14, 2007. www.alternet.org/water/70475/big_coal%27s_dirty_plans_for_our_energy_future_%28with_shocking_photos%29.

Clean Energy Digest, "Stop the Wind Madness," November 14, 2007. www.cleanenergydigest.com/2007/11/14/stop-the-wind-madness.

———, "The Murky World of Nuclear Energy," December 3, 2007. www.cleanenergydigest.com/2007/12/03/the-murky-world-of-nuclear-energy.

Blythe Copeland, "How to Go Green: Alternative Energy," Planet Green, January 27, 2009. http://planetgreen.discovery.com/go-green/alternative-energy/index.html.

Murray Dobbin, "Corny Energy 'Solution'" *The Tyee*, April 10, 2007. http://thetyee.ca/Views/2007/04/04/CornEnergy.

Rachel Dowd, "Life After Oil," Conscious Choice, April 2009. www.lime.com/magazines?uri=consciouschoice.com/lime/2009/04/lifeafteroil0904.html.

Edison Electric Institute, "Keep Our Fuel Mix Diverse: What's the Fuel Mix Where I Live?" Get Energy Active, 2008. www.getenergyactive.org/fuel/state.htm.

Michael Kanellos, "Shrinking the Cost for Solar Power," CNET News, May 11, 2007. http://news.cnet.com/Shrinking-the-cost-for-solar-power/2100-11392_3-6182947.html.

Michael T. Klare, "The Energy Challenge of Our Lifetime," TomDispatch, November 9, 2008. www.tomdispatch.com/post/175000/michael_klare_the_energy_challenge_of_our_lifetime.

Thomas Lifson, "Problems with 'Green' Energy You May Not Have Heard About," *American Thinker*, December 26, 2008. www.americanthinker.com/blog/2008/12/problems_with_green_energy_you.html.

Tara Lohan, "Wind vs. Coal: False Choices in the Battle to Resolve Our Energy Crisis," AlterNet, February 15, 2007. www.alternet.org/environment/47997/wind_vs._coal%3A_false_choices_in_the_battle_to_resolve_our_energy_crisis.

Franz Matzner, "Climate Facts: Putting Biofuels on the Right Track," Natural Resources Defense Council, April 2008. www.nrdc.org/air/transportation/biofuels/track.pdf.

Darryl McMahon, "The Hydrogen Economy: An Idea Whose Time Hasn't Come," Econogics, July 15, 2008. www.econogics.com/en/heconomy.htm.

Terrence McNally, "America Has Oil on the Brain," AlterNet, May 17, 2007. www.alternet.org/environment/51758/america_has_oil_on_the_brain.

David Morris, "Green, at Any Cost?" *Irregular*, February 18, 2009. www.theirregular.com/news/2009/0218/op_ed/013.html.

MoveBeyondOil, "Myths, Facts, and Solutions," 2009. http://movebeyondoil.org/index_files/Page561.htm.

National Geographic, "Biofuels Compared," 2009. http://ngm.nationalgeographic.com/2007/10/biofuels/biofuels-interactive.

Our-Energy, "Geothermal Energy Facts." www.our-energy.com/energy_facts/geothermal_energy_facts.html.

Frank Paynter, "Solar Power, Solar Panels, Solar Poison," Super Eco, January 22, 2009. www.supereco.com/news/2009/01/22/solar-power-solar-panels-solar-poison.

Neal Peirce, "Global Warming Cures: Time to Harvest Ocean Power?" Stateline, July 30, 2006. www.stateline.org/live/printable/story?contentId=129949.

Manila Ryce, "Biofuel Is Still a Stupid Idea," AlterNet, May 13, 2008. www.alternet.org/blogs/environment/85222/biofuel_is_still_a_stupid_idea.

Michael Schirber, "Whatever Happened to Wind Energy?" LiveScience, January 14, 2008. www.livescience.com/environment/080114-wind-energy.html.

———, "5 Myths About Wind Energy," LiveScience, September 24, 2008. www.livescience.com/environment/ 080924-pf-wind-energy.html.

Peter Slavin, "How Wind Farms May Really Replace Coal Mining," AlterNet, August 19, 2008. www.alternet.org/environment/95535/how_wind_farms_may_really_replace_coal_mining.

Peter Teague and Jeff Navin, "Global Warming in an Age of Energy Anxiety," American Prospect, June 26, 2007. http://prospect.org/cs/articles?article=global_warming_in_an_age_of_energy_anxiety.

Union of Concerned Scientists, "Clean Energy 101," August 28, 2008. www.ucsusa.org/clean_energy/clean_energy_101.

U.S. Department of Energy Office of Energy Efficiency and Renewable Energy, "Energy Savers," May 20, 2009. www.energysavers.gov.

———, "The Green Power Network," July 7, 2009. http://apps3.eere.energy.gov/greenpower.

———, "Fuel Economy," July 23, 2009. www.fueleconomy.gov.

Bill Vitek, "These Revolutionary Times," Prairie Writers Circle, August 27, 2008. www.landinstitute.org/vnews/display.v/ART/2008/08/20/48ac6411eeda8.